MORNING
coffee

MORNING

coffee

Highly Caffeinated Daily Recovery

New York Times Best Selling Author
MICHAEL GRAUBART

For my Mom, who taught me to play Scrabble

MAY I START SOMETHING FOR YOU?

I don't know you, but I love you.

You might ask, how can that be?

Of course I know you and love you, and of course you know me. Recovery works because addicts and alcoholics are interchangeable under the skin.

You're reading these words because you're hoping to find something that will make your life better. You're reading these words because you like the idea of having a fun, thoughtful way to get your day going.

And you're reading these words because you are doing one of the hardest things that any human being can do—staying clean, sober, or abstinent, as you define it, a day at a time, an hour at a time, or maybe even a breath at a time.

That's why I love you.

And I'm over here doing the same thing. I attended my first meeting on August 25, 1987, an Al-Anon meeting with an Adult Child of Alcoholics focus, in Cambridge, Massachusetts.

It was just after my twenty-ninth birthday, and yet again, I had been devastated by the alcoholic behavior of a family member.

My sisters, who had gotten sober by then, understood what I was going through, and they sent me to Al-Anon.

That first meeting was a revelation. Forty different people were all sharing bits and pieces of my story. It felt as if they had all grown up in my home, or homes like my home. I felt a sense of identification, connection, and belonging. I was so blown away that the next day I didn't even have the strength to get out of bed.

That began a recovery journey, first in Al-Anon, and then in Alcoholics Anonymous starting in 1992, and then in Debtors Anonymous starting two years after that, with forays into other programs as well, including Overeaters Anonymous and S.L.A.A.

Today, at twenty-seven years sober and thirty-one years in Al-Anon, I'm as active as ever in recovery, going to meetings, sponsoring others, and working my own program.

I'm fascinated by 12-Step recovery. Whenever I think about its origins, I recall the Elton John song, *Candle In The Wind*, because the idea of creating a movement that would one day keep millions of people clean, sober, and abstinent—including you and me—well, doesn't that sound like trying to light a candle in the wind?

But that's exactly what our co-founders did, and that's exactly what we get to share with the newcomer.

About me? I like to say that I overcame every advantage on my way to the bottom. I grew up in a beautiful home in a lovely suburb. Our house was so pretty that my aunt, who was a designer and decorator, actually got our home featured in *Brides Magazine* when I was fifteen years old. That same year, the wheels came off in our family. Alcoholism, infidelity, drug abuse, unwanted pregnancy, even murder. On the outside, we had it all together, and *I* had it all together. On the inside, it was something else again.

I graduated from a top college, went to a seminary abroad, worked in New York, and then graduated from one of the top law schools in the United States. Within eighteen months of getting my J.D. degree, my legal career was over, due to drinking and a terrible attitude. A year after that came my introduction to 12-Step recovery, and I've been doing the drill pretty much ever since.

I'm a big fan of one-day-at-a-time books, whether it's the Al-Anon *ODAAT*, the Hazelden *24 Hours* book, or *As Bill Sees It*. But I thought there might be room for a book that served people of all addictions—and that I might be the right person to write it, since I definitely qualify for, and have benefitted from, so many different fellowships.

Today, my life works. I'm married, I have four wonderful children, I'm successful in my chosen field (not law), and as I was promised when I came into recovery, I am indeed relatively comfortable most of the time. Nobody could accuse me of living in a state of serenity, but considering the stresses and strains of modern living, I do OK.

I learned to be a businessperson in recovery, and in this book, in addition to the 12-Step messages, I've also got some ideas for you about life that come from some of the top motivational speakers, entrepreneurial coaches, and other folks whose work typically does not make it into conference approved literature.

My hope is that you find in these pages inspiration, hope, and even an expectation that great things will happen in your life. Recovery is not a shield against tragedy and misfortune. It just means that there are far fewer self-inflicted wounds, and then when difficult things come along, we can get through them.

I'm hoping, with this book, that we can get through them together.

I was newly sober at a meeting in Knoxville, Tennessee, where I heard for the first time, "If nobody else tells you 'I love you' today, then '*I* love you.'"

I'd like to pass that message along right now. If nobody tells you 'I love you' today, then please be certain that *I* love you. And even though I don't know you, I know you.

So let's get this party started.

JANUARY 1
The Only New Year's Resolution Worth Making

*E*verybody talks about making New Year's resolutions, but how many of us actually do so?

I can simplify things for you. There's really only one New Year's resolution worth making, and here it is: *Don't lie to yourself.* We bury ourselves alive under piles of lies. As a result, we cannot reach our true potential. I'm going to share with you the three primary lies that we tell ourselves that keep us locked in discomfort, if not outright misery.

Lie #1—*It's not that bad.* Tell yourself the truth. If it really is that bad, then you'll make a change and do something about it. But if you keep telling yourself that you can live with the problem, that it's not the end of the world, and so on, you'll never make a change.

Lie #2—*It can't get any better.* Actually, anything can get better if you take the right Steps or have the right attitude. Action and acceptance transform practically everything.

Lie #3—*I can't because I'm…*fill in the blank (*Too old, too young, too busy, not smart enough, discriminated against,* whatever.) Don't play the age, gender, or race card against yourself. You can do anything that other people can do.

"Don't lie to me!"

JANUARY 2
Rules, Rules, Rules

Our brains are wired to find rules to live by, because rules create consistency, certainty, and a comforting sense of control. The problem comes when we try to live with other people, because they have their own rules, which are often in conflict with ours.

Now that we're clean and sober, we are no longer simply trying to apply our rules to everyone around us, or letting other people dominate us with their rulebook. Instead, it's my responsibility as a sober individual to examine each unconscious rule as it surfaces and ask, "How important is it?" If the rule really matters to me, I have to stand up for it. But chances are, it's negotiable. It's not that big of a deal. There may be no reason at all for doing things in a particular way other than the fact that "that's how I've always done it."

When you're having a dispute with another human being, you're probably just having a dispute over whose rule wins.

The next time you're having a dispute with a loved one, you probably aren't arguing with the person—you're arguing with his or her rules. That's why it's so important to examine our rules and determine whether we really need to keep enforcing them.

A little flexibility goes a long way.

JANUARY 3
Just Do Exactly One Push-up

Still hung up on New Year's resolutions? A fitness expert once told me that January 20 was "Reality Day" at gyms. That's the day when the New Year's resolutions people made their final appearances... until the following January 1. "Their intentions are in the right place," she said, "but the goals they've set for themselves are just a little too extreme."

Author and financial and business authority Lee Brower has a better way. "Get dressed, go to the gym, and do one push-up," he counsels. "Then you can go home. Or do one minute on the treadmill. Or swim one lap in the pool."

Lee is talking, of course, about the magic of setting ludicrously attainable goals. The reality, he says, is that once you do your one push-up, or your one minute on the treadmill, or your one lap, you won't stop. But if you tell yourself you're going to do one hundred push-ups, or swim a mile, or whatever, the first day, you're probably just setting yourself up for failure.

That's why we don't try to stay clean and sober for a year at a time, a month at a time, or even a week at a time. A day at a time is just the right measure. Because if you get one day, you can almost certainly get two. And then you're on your way.

Think small.

JANUARY 4
"No" Is a Complete Sentence

It's amazing how alcoholics and addicts, strong enough to withstand the ill effects of our drugs of choice, have a hard time standing up for ourselves. Maybe it's the way we were raised. But a lot of the time, we find it hard to do what then First Lady Nancy Reagan advised a long time ago—*just say no.*

We feel that we have to justify our behavior, good, bad, or indifferent, to other people—whether it's parents, children, bosses, sometimes complete strangers. We find it almost impossible to stand up for ourselves if there's something we don't want to do or that we know we shouldn't do.

The good news is that "No" is a complete sentence. If you say no, that's it. You don't have to answer with an explanation or a negotiation. Don't let other people bully you into changing your mind or defending how you feel. If you don't want to do it, or you shouldn't do it, or doing it is the wrong thing, just say no.

Your no is enough.

JANUARY 5
Come On, Not the Penny Again!

Sometimes when I'm sharing some disappointment or unhappiness with my Boston sponsor Charlie M., he tells me to take a penny out of my pocket and read it to him.

"Liberty?" I ask. He shakes his head. "United States of America?" He shakes his head again.

"In God We Trust?"

Charlie nods. "Exactly," he says.

It doesn't say "In God we understand," or "In God we always get exactly what we want, from the parking space to cash and prizes." Instead, we simply trust that our Higher Power has our best interests at heart, and if we trust in that Higher Power, we'll either get what we want or we will intuitively understand how to handle that which we don't like.

At some point, the Federal Government will take the penny out of circulation. If that ever happens, be sure to hang onto a penny and keep it in your pocket. That way, you can remind yourself that you have a Higher Power you may not always understand, or even like, but one that you can always trust.

E. Pluribus You.

JANUARY 6
There's No Such Thing as a Bad Day

Sometimes people talk about having "a bad day." In reality, they usually just had an unpleasant moment on an otherwise normal day. The old-timers taught that you could start your day over anytime, just by hitting your knees and telling your Higher Power you want to start fresh.

Off to a bad start with your spouse, partner, parent, or child? Hit your knees and start the day over. Bad first hour at work? Sneak off to the bathroom, hit your knees, and talk to your HP.

The good thing about being sober is that you never have to have a bad day—because anytime it looks like you're having one, you can just hit the reset button. When I was drinking, the "reset button" meant getting hammered. This is a much better way to take a mulligan.

Better to restart your day than your day count.

JANUARY 7
Need, Greed, and Speed

Those are the three drivers from the lives of most practicing (and many recovering) addicts and alcoholics.

Need—We feel ourselves motivated by a sense of compulsion to do more, accomplish more, and generally make up for lost time.

Greed—We struggle with the concept of "enough," seldom believing that we are enough, that we have enough, or that we do enough.

Speed—Everything has to happen now, now, now.

The good thing about sobriety is that it offers addicts and alcoholics a much-needed alternative to need, greed, and speed. Instead of living in a world of wants, we learn to become content with what we have. Instead of being dominated by money, power, and possessions, we feel a sense of *enough*, perhaps for the first time. And because we pray and meditate, or sit quietly in a meeting, listening to the speakers or our own thoughts, we learn to pause when agitated, instead of rushing headlong into whatever comes next.

Out go need, greed, and speed.
In come cool, calm, and collected.

JANUARY 8
"I'm Bad, I'm Bad, I'm Bad...
They Found Out."

Alcoholics and addicts often labor under a terrible burden of self-hatred. Somehow we cross the line from understanding that we did bad things to concluding that we are bad people. Fortunately, the program comes along to remind us that we are not bad people getting good; we are sick people getting well.

Nevertheless, we're always waiting for that other shoe to drop. We live in a sense of dread that people will finally see just how bad we really are. When they do, it almost comes as a relief, because we don't have to keep pretending that we're good.

Newsflash: there's nothing bad about you. You are a beautiful child of God, who wants the best for you, loves you, and does not create junk. If you don't believe me, look in the mirror. I mean, *really look*. And say, "I love you." Do that as often as you need to until you finally start to believe it.

You're awesome. Deal with it.

JANUARY 9
I Think I Need Another Meeting to Get Over How I Felt at This Meeting

*O*nce, I was setting up chairs at an Al-Anon meeting, while a perfectly healthy looking fellow sat splendidly in a chair I had set out, not offering to help. Only after I had set up the whole room, my resentment dialed up to eleven, did I see his crutches leaning against the wall behind him. Oops.

And then there was a time the woman leading the meeting told what seemed like an elaborate shaggy dog story about how she had driven forty minutes to a therapy session, on three straight occasions, only to find that the door was locked. *Get to the point*, I said to myself, writhing with impatience.

Then she explained, "When I got there the fourth time, I turned the knob in the opposite direction. It turns out that if I had done that on any of my previous visits, I would have gotten in. I just couldn't bring myself to ask for help."

Give people a break.

JANUARY 10
"I Got Sober, and Everybody Else Changed."

When we get clean and sober, we begin to see everyone else in a different light. Instead of projecting our own negative self-image onto them, we see others as who they really are—beautiful children of God. And that's how we begin to see ourselves.

It's often said that other people recognize our growth sooner than we do. In early sobriety, we go through subtle transformations—we look less tired, there's more light in our eyes, and—it can happen—we even smile.

So it makes sense that while we might not see our own growth, we see everyone around us changing. Are they really any different? Probably not, but our perceptions of them changed as our perception of ourselves changed.

Why couldn't they have been this nice when
I was still drinking and using?

JANUARY 11
People Who Don't Go to Meetings ...

... *d*on't find out what happens to people who don't go to meetings.

How do people become "12-Step trivia questions?" As in "Do you remember so-and-so?" Because they went back to drinking and using. It's not as though people who relapse text the secretary of their home group to say "I went out." But word gets around. We start looking around for that person, and then we hear that the person in question relapsed, beat up his or her spouse, went back to jail, or died.

My late, beloved sponsor Milton D., used to call one guy "Scout" because he came back repeatedly from relapses "with arrows in his behind." At least he came back.

Do you really want to be the person in your home group that,
six months after you picked up, no one even remembers?

JANUARY 12
Did You Grow Up, or Just Get Big?

Can we really associate the term "grown ups" with practicing addicts and alcoholics? Not if we're being honest. The truth is that in our hometowns, we didn't grow up. All we did was get big.

Growing up implies emotional and spiritual growth. Getting big just means reaching the biological age and physical size that allows us to drive a car, go to the liquor store, or text the dealer.

Recovery is an engine of spiritual growth, but only if I put the work in. If all I do is go to meetings, date newcomers, and avoid the Steps, I'm going to remain in the same childish state I've inhabited for so many years. The point of recovery is not to become the world's oldest teenager. Instead, the goal is to allow our spiritual and emotional development to match our adult appearance.

Go big spiritually…or stay home.

JANUARY 13
Love For Sale

A lot of people have the mistaken belief that a love relationship is a 50/50 proposition—you do your 50%, and I'll do my 50%, and everything will be fine. In reality, that's not how it goes. However much or however little we do, we find ourselves glaring at the other person and asking, "Where's *my* 50?"

We might even be more generous and say, "My relationship is 90/10—I do 90%, and I only expect 10% in return." But if we're expecting *anything* back from the other person, then we've put a price tag on our love and affection. This has another name: prostitution.

The best way to ensure that your relationship will work is to make it a 100/0 affair, where you give 100% and you expect nothing in return. You have to be almost superhuman to do that, but this is the goal. When we do something for the other person simply because it's the right thing to do, because we love that person, and because you want to show affection, appreciation, and attention, it's amazing how much more we get back.

There's nothing 50/50 about love.

JANUARY 14
They'll Get You Loaded Before You Get Them Sober

When Alcoholics Anonymous sends its members to make a "12-Step call"—a visit on a member who is still drinking, the sober alcoholics go in pairs. That's because the drinker can persuade the sober alcoholic to start drinking again.

Sometimes numerous sober addicts and alcoholics want to prove to themselves and their drinking buddies just how strong their program really is. So they go to the bar or the club, certain that the protection of their Higher Power will be enough to keep them from drinking and using, while everyone else is getting hammered. What can go wrong?

Twelve-Step recovery is powerful, but it's really not enough to keep us clean and sober when we put ourselves into positions of real danger—any situation where *they* are still drinking and *we* are not. Often, the motivation is the desire to keep one's friends. Alas, if your friends drink and use and you've got no drugs or alcohol to share with them, they won't be your friends for very long.

I told you so.

JANUARY 15
Your Picture Is on
Your Higher Power's Refrigerator

Until I had children, I really didn't understand just how much my Higher Power loved me.

If you have children, you know what I'm talking about. Even when they're at their most annoying, you still love them and want the best for them. So ask not how you feel about your Higher Power. Instead, ask how your Higher Power feels about you.

Anyone with the slightest amount of intellectual honesty would have to say that their Creator wants the best for them. It doesn't mean your HP wants the easiest life for you, or that your definition of what's best for you matches your Higher Power's. As Garth Brooks sang, in country music's greatest triple negative lyric, "Just because He don't answer don't mean He don't care."

God must have a very big refrigerator so as to fit all of our photos on it, but if God can create the universe, he can certainly create a big fridge.

God doesn't have grandchildren.

JANUARY 16
No, You Don't Get a Tip for Making Change

I went to my local coffee shop and bought a bottle of water. I paid the barista with cash, and she gave me a meaningful glance as she handed me my change. She wasn't signaling me to ask for her phone number. Instead, she was asking with her eyes for a tip.

Traditionally, tips are earned when a service is provided—driving a cab, cleaning a hotel room, waiting tables. But you don't get a tip for making change if that's your job. That's just an attitude of entitlement, which strikes alcoholics and addicts with even greater frequency than it does baristas.

Many of us addicts and alcoholics simply feel entitled to, well, everything. But that's not how the world works. Some of us might have been spoiled by our parents or we might have had special skills—athletic, scholastic, or otherwise—that caused people to fawn over us.

But here in the real world, you have to earn stuff. In the program, the acronym T.I.M.E. stands for "Things I Must Earn." You can't get a one year chip in ninety days, but you can make any dream come true if you really work for it.

Here's a tip—don't be entitled.

JANUARY 17
In Al-Anon, Our "Drink" Has Two Legs

To qualify for Al-Anon, you must have been affected by the drinking or sobriety of a human being, living or dead. The effect of someone else's alcoholism on a person is often devastating. It destroys self-esteem, creates endless conflict with authority figures, and generally sets that person up for a lot of challenges in life.

The good news is that the 12 Steps create a spiritual change in the alcoholic, and induces a similar spiritual shift in those affected by the alcoholism of others. Or, as we say in Al-Anon, there's hope and there's help, and you don't have to go on hurting the way you've been hurting.

The primary manifestation of the Al-Anon condition ("Al-Anon" is *not* a disease, no matter what you might have heard) is an addiction to relationships, often with people who are not good for us. We find people who act hurtfully. We get excited and become convinced that we can change them. We fail, of course, and hilarity does not ensue.

Can you give up an addiction to unhealthy relationships with emotionally unhealthy people? If you go to Al-Anon, you sure can.

You can stay sober without also going to Al-Anon,
but it won't be much fun.

JANUARY 18
Your Ego Is Not Your Amigo

E.G.O. stands for "Edging God Out." Ego says things like, "I can figure it out all by myself."

That's an appropriate attitude if you're a five-year-old, but not if you're trying to be a functioning adult.

Ego says "I don't need anybody's advice because my opinion is good enough." That's not true. As my sponsor Milton used to say, "Dictators have yes men, but statesmen have advisors." What usually happens to dictators? Everything is terrific, until they are deposed and disposed of. What happens to statesmen and stateswomen? They're honored in this lifetime and remembered long after they're gone.

The problem with having a big ego is it leaves very little space for everyone else in your life. It's hard to have great relationships with other people if you're busy sucking up all the oxygen in the room.

Ego is the Latin word for *I*. Can you be successful running your life on high octane ego?

Tough to be happy when you can't play well with others.

JANUARY 19
Row, Row, Row Your Boat

*M*y sponsor, Milton, used to remind us that the song says, "Row, row, row your boat"—not your wife's boat, not your kid's boat, not your boss's boat.

And then where do you row it? "Gently down the stream." Or, as Milton would say, "Not paddling furiously against the current."

The Big Book of Alcoholics Anonymous says, "See what you can pack into the stream of life." It doesn't say, "Fight your way upstream."

And why do we do all this? Because "Life is but a dream."

Milton also used to quote a Buddhist parable that life is like falling off a cliff—you can either panic and grab for the shoots and branches as you plummet, or you can just kick back and enjoy the ride, because you're going to end up in the same place either way.

Merrily, merrily, merrily, merrily.

JANUARY 20
Did You Know That Your Smartphone ... Is a Phone?

I saw a news story with a headline that said, "On Smartphones, The Least Used App...Is The Phone."

It's true. Today, people will text, instant message, WhatsApp, or otherwise reach out with one app or another. But actually pick up the phone? You mean I have to *talk* to somebody? And see how they are? Can't I just get to the point with a text?

I ask my sponsees not to text me. I explain to them that I cannot tell the tone of voice from a text. Also, I'd like to think that the program deserves a little more than the 2.6 seconds it takes to type out a four word text to one's sponsor. Instead, let's find out what's really going on.

Before the advent of smartphones, A.A. had a term for getting drunk, picking up the phone, calling people, and exhausting them with our alcoholic rambling. We called it "Black Cord Fever." Today, smartphones don't have cords, but they still have phones. And so does your sponsor's smartphone. So do the smart thing, and use your smartphone's phone. You will end up having a better day.

Reach out and touch someone.

JANUARY 21
Everything in Recovery Takes Six Months and Twenty Minutes

Alcoholics and addicts, both practicing and recovering, are great at procrastination. Why do today what we can put off till tomorrow, we reason. Or as a college friend used to say, "The sooner I fall behind, the more time I have to catch up."

The problem is that we live in a "now" world. When you want something, when do you want it? Sometime next week? No—you want immediate delivery. As Carrie Fisher wrote in *Postcards From the Edge*, "Instant gratification takes too long."

So instead of waiting six months to find a sponsor, start taking the Steps, get a job, or make an amend, why not do it right now? The thing that you're putting off will probably just take twenty minutes, and then it's behind you—and your life is better. Why wait? You're only going to get something better out of the deal anyway.

How do you handle procrastination? Put it off.

JANUARY 22
Rejection Is God's Protection

This is a classic program phrase that old-timers tell newcomers who feel bitterly disappointed because the person they wanted to date, or just sleep with, said no.

In the moment, it's frustrating when we don't get the specific outcome we had been hoping for, whether that meant a new relationship, a new job, a new apartment, or a shorter sentence. It is up to our sponsors to remind us that maybe your Higher Power has something better for you in mind. Bill W. used to say that "The good is the enemy of the best."

So the next time you don't get what you want, you can either play the old Rolling Stones song by the same name and remember that you will get what you need, or remind yourself that maybe there's a good reason for the rejection that you can't understand right now. So don't quit before the miracle happens.

Rejection is a bitter pill.
But don't wash it down with Budweiser.

JANUARY 23
Don't Pull Up the Ladder!

It breaks my heart when I hear old-timers say, "I stopped going to meetings because I got sick of listening to newcomers." Those old-timers should have just stayed in the meetings and talked more, leaving less time for the newcomers to speak!

I keep coming back, after all these years, because I love the program and because I know I'm not "cured." (Only ham is cured; we just get a daily reprieve.) At the same time, I know I have an obligation not to pull up the ladder because there are still plenty of newcomers trying to get their foot on the first rung.

May I help you?

JANUARY 24
The Denial Is Bigger Than the Disease

"I'm not that bad." "I can take it." "I only drink or use on days that end in Y." "A.A. is for quitters."

The excuses people make about their alcoholism or addictions are endless. Unfortunately, you can't scare or manipulate addicts and alcoholics into recognizing the true nature of their situations. Instead, we can pray for them, but we must wait for them to realize they need help. In short, there's a lot we can do about the disease, but there's precious little we can do about the denial.

If you are new to a 12-Step program, it's because on some level, something cracked *your* denial. You have a unique opportunity that may not ever come again in your life to handle your addiction. If you take it, good things will happen. If you don't take advantage, and you pick up again, there's nothing to keep that wall of denial from growing ever taller and separating you, perhaps permanently, from recovery, or even life itself.

Don't just keep coming back. Stay.

JANUARY 25
Get Off the Cross; We Need the Wood

*O*h, how alcoholics and addicts love to be martyrs. We're never so happy as when we're abjectly miserable, complaining to anyone who will listen—and those people get harder and harder to find as the night goes on—that our miserable lives are everybody else's fault.

Martyr is actually the Greek word for *witness*. In other words, if you've turned yourself into a martyr, you're barely living. You're just witnessing other people's lives. The good thing about sobriety is that instead of simply witnessing what other people are doing to your life, you get to have a say in the outcome of your own life. Doesn't that sound like it's a lot more fun?

Nobody likes martyrs.

JANUARY 26
If God Is Your Co-Pilot, You're in the Wrong Seat

Years ago, there was a famous book, and then an even more famous movie, called *God Is My Co-Pilot*. It told the story of an aging fighter pilot who gets the chance to fly with a famous Chinese squadron. In 12-Step land, however, we like to say that we put God in the pilot's seat. So if you're sitting in God's seat, piloting your own life, you may want to move over.

Dr. Paul, who wrote the story including the passage on acceptance, used to say that sobriety is like riding a two-seater bicycle, with God in the front seat steering and him in the back seat pedaling. Dr. Paul said that he would tap God on the shoulder and ask where they were going, to which God would just smile and say, "Keep pedaling."

So whatever means of transportation—planes or bicycles—floats your boat, the main thing is to let God steer.

Enjoy the ride.

JANUARY 27
My Disease Is Packed in Grease and I Can Reassemble It in the Dark

An old-timer named Doc, sober forty years, frequently uttered that phrase at my home group in Lynn, Massachusetts. Packed in grease—just like a weapon. And just like a weapon, I could use it against others, or I could turn it around and point it at myself.

And reassemble it in the dark? That tells me that we're so practiced at alcoholism or addiction that it would take no effort to start drinking and using again. One flimsy excuse, and I would be off and running.

I've been sober for a few twenty-four hours, as the old-timers used to say, but my disease is still packed in grease, and I'm sure that my reassembly skills are undiminished. What stands between me and cleaning, unholstering, and firing that weapon of destruction?

The 12 Steps, my Higher Power, and the fellowship and program of Alcoholics Anonymous. That's about it.

No one can make you drink or use without your permission.

JANUARY 28
A Grateful Heart Never Drinks

Practicing addicts and alcoholics are competitive, though typically, they are only competing with people who are doing better than they are. What's the point of comparing your life with somebody who's doing worse? The whole point of comparison, for addicts and alkies, is to make ourselves feel so bad that we have to go drink or use.

My sponsor Milton used to say that the only valid comparison we can make is how we are doing now versus how we were doing when we were still drinking and using.

By contrast, gratitude is the magic elixir that makes it unnecessary to pick up a drink, a drug, or a substitute. Most practicing addicts and alcoholics don't want to feel grateful, because if they feel grateful, they won't want to use, and then where will they be?

So the question isn't just whether you want to stop drinking or using. The question is whether you want to stop being unhappy. And remarkably, tons of alcoholics and addicts are perfectly content being miserable. I hope you're not one of them.

Yes, you can be grateful for being grateful.

JANUARY 29
Don't Give Your Problems Too Much Oxygen

This is something my late grand-sponsor, Bob H., used to say: "Don't give your problems too much oxygen, because you'll have a whole new set in ninety days." Most of the things that trouble alcoholics and addicts aren't life threatening illnesses or world peace. Instead, we're just bummed because we need a place to live, we've got bills, we had a fight with our ex, or other mundane matters.

How we love to turn molehills into mountains, and small mountains into Kilimanjaros. The reality is that whatever we're facing, there will be a resolution. It may not be exactly what we want, but ninety days from now, we may not even remember that the problem existed. So if it's not going to affect you ninety days from now, or five years from now, why are you so upset about it today?

Don't give your problems breathing room.

JANUARY 30
Players and Fans in 12-Step Recovery

*I*n practically every 12-Step meeting, you can divide the room into players and fans. Players are the people who are serious about the program of Alcoholics Anonymous—they're sitting up front, they're sharing, they're taking commitments, talking to newcomers…in short, they're getting better and enjoying themselves. By contrast, the fans typically sit in the "slipper seats" in the back (so called because people who sit in them often slip out) and critique everything about the meeting. The coffee's weak. The sharing's boring. The whole thing is stupid.

As Clancy I., the legendary founder of the Pacific Group, has said, "There's a battle for the heart and soul of the newcomer between the people in the meeting and the people smoking outside the meeting."

The problem is that some of those smokers win that battle. It's not enough to get close to an A.A. meeting, or stand in front of an A.A. meeting, or even sit in the back of an A.A. meeting in those "slipper seats." Stick with the winners. Sit up front. Stick your hand out. Let us save your life. You only have to do this once, so you might as well be a player and not a fan.

"The credit belongs to the man who is actually in the arena."
—Theodore Roosevelt

JANUARY 31
The Contract in the 3rd Step Prayer

When my first A.A. sponsor, Hal R., got me to the 3rd Step, he challenged me to locate the contract embedded in the 3rd Step prayer. "Not one alcoholic in fifty finds it," he said. "You won't be the one, but you might as well look for it."

I couldn't find it, so Hal pointed it out to me. It comes in the second half of the 3rd Step prayer, which reads, "Take away my difficulties, that victory over them may bear witness to those I would help of Thy Power, Thy Love, and Thy Way of life."

The contract: God's job is to keep on taking away my difficulties. My job—to bear witness—or just simply to tell—those I would help (my fellow alcoholics) that God was in fact taking away my difficulties. And God would keep taking away my difficulties as long as I kept on telling people that that's what God was doing.

I can affirm that God has been taking away my difficulties ever since I joined Alcoholics Anonymous. And if you let Him, He'll do the same thing for you, too.

God keeps His word.

FEBRUARY 1
How to Make Your Home Group Laugh Their Heads Off

There are three little words you can say that will cause your home group to burst into peals of laughter. Want to know what they are? Here goes:

"I've been thinking."

Twelve-Step programs offer newcomers an opportunity to check their thinking against that of people with more sober time, or the group as a whole. It's actually very sweet when a newcomer shares his or her romantic, business, or travel plans at the group level, only to look bewildered when the group responds with empathetic laughter.

I can't really say "They're not laughing at you—they're laughing with you," because they *are* laughing at you. Honestly, they're laughing at themselves, because they remember when they put forth the same ideas, either to their sponsors or to the group as a whole.

If you want to make God laugh, tell Him your plans. It turns out that you can make your home group laugh doing exactly the same thing.

If you're going for hysterics, tell them, "I found her."

FEBRUARY 2
Actually, You _Can_ Watch
the Super Bowl Clean and Sober

The Super Bowl is a perfectly good excuse for getting loaded, but we addicts and alcoholics never needed excuses. It's just that it somehow seems more socially acceptable to get drunk on Super Bowl Sunday than almost any other day of the year.

Here's the shocking truth about the Super Bowl—not only can you watch it sober, but if you do, you will remember who won.

This may not seem like that big of a deal, and in the grand scheme of things, remembering where you watched the Super Bowl is setting a fairly low goal for yourself in life. The good news is that your home group may well sponsor a Super Bowl party, where folks will get together, enjoy the game without alcohol or drugs, and not punch each other in the parking lot during halftime.

So ask around. See if you can find a sober Super Bowl party. Those parties were proof to many of us when we were new that we actually could enjoy life without a beer, a bong, or a bump.

A sober Stanley Cup finals? Probably too much to ask.

FEBRUARY 3
If You Aren't Fifteen Minutes Early, You're Late

The old-timers used to say, "If you don't get to your meeting fifteen minutes early, you're late. And if you leave within fifteen minutes after the meeting ended, you left early." They wanted us to have time to get to know people, talk about whatever was going on, make friends, maybe even find a new person you can help.

You might think that you don't have all that much to offer because you haven't been clean that long, or maybe you've been coming for a long time, but you haven't amassed a lot of sober time. But sometimes people just need to talk—they need someone to listen. So you can be that empathetic listener for someone newer than yourself.

There's really nothing like 12-Step programs to break down the walls between strangers. As *The Big Book* says, "We are people who ordinarily would not mix."

But once we do, most of us get along great. So show up early, stay late, and put yourself in the middle of the pack.

You give us thirty minutes,
we'll relieve your misery and loneliness.

FEBRUARY 4
You Only <u>Have</u> to Go to Meetings until You <u>Want</u> to Go

"*H*ow long do I have to go to these stupid meetings?" the newcomer asks.

"You only *have* to go," responds the crusty old-timer, "until you *want* to go. Then you don't have to go anymore."

Twelve-Step recovery may feel like a punishment…but after a while, you realize that it's actually a privilege. You sit in a folding chair in a church basement, you put a buck in the basket, or maybe nothing, and the biggest problem of your life goes away. On top of that, people ask you out for coffee, and they even pay.

The second best meeting I've ever been to is the most recent meeting I've been to. The best meeting is the one I'm going to next.

Even if you don't want to go, you still have to go.

FEBRUARY 5
They Don't Want <u>Your</u> Money; They Want <u>Their</u> Money

*T*he Big Book says that alcoholics, and by extension most addicts, typically owe money. What a shocker! We borrowed money and didn't pay it back! These may include credit card bills, child support, alimony, or taxes. But creditors don't want *your* money. They want *their* money. It's just that you happen to have it. Or more likely, you don't have it, and are wondering how you're going to get it.

In Debtors Anonymous, we learn to reach out to our creditors and explain to them that we don't have *their* money just now, but we'd like to work out a payment plan. It's a lot easier to be proactive and explain your situation to the credit card company, the bank, or the court—than to wait for them to come after you with some scary looking legal documents.

Bankruptcy is like liposuction—it might transform things for the moment, but it doesn't address the underlying habits. So reach out to your creditors and work things out.

Life is like a s@!# sandwich—the more bread you have,
the less s@!# you have to eat.

FEBRUARY 6
Wanting to Be Important in Alcoholics Anonymous...

...*i*s like wanting to be head leper in a leper colony.

My sponsor, Milton, used to say that it's important to be well liked in A.A. That's because in A.A., people really know you. They know if you're serious about recovery or not.

If you're so obnoxious that even the people in A.A. or your 12-Step program can't stand you, that's a bad sign.

This doesn't mean that you have to like everyone in your meetings, however. If you do like everyone in all of your meetings, you probably aren't going to enough meetings.

So quit trying to be head leper and start being a regular leper. You'll be happier, and so will the rest of us.

Go be important somewhere else.

FEBRUARY 7
Every Character Defect Has a Payoff

"You must get something out of being angry," an old-timer told me once, "because you're angry a lot." Of course, when he said that, that made me angry.

Step 6 asks whether we're willing to give up the character defects, or as my sponsor calls them, bad habits, that we've identified in Steps 4 and 5. But what does that really mean?

Every character defect has a payoff. When I'm angry, I have a power rush. I feel invincible. Envy is my sense of justice, because it's not fair if that guy has so much and I have so little. Fear has a payoff—it's like watching a scary movie without having to pay for Netflix.

So when we get to Step 6, what we're really asking is, "Am I willing to give up the benefit or payoff that comes from each of the character defects or bad habits I enumerated in Steps 4 and 5?"

Your life is your fault.

FEBRUARY 8
Are You Willing to Be Willing to Be Willing?

This is the ultimate 12-Step trick question. Typically, the sponsee calls the sponsor, the sponsee then describes a resentment, and the sponsor asks, "Would you be willing to release that resentment to your Higher Power?" or words to that effect.

Sometimes the sponsee says yes, but not always. Now what?

"Would you be willing to be willing?" the sponsor asks. Meaning, are you open to the idea that even if you are not willing right now, you might get willing at some point? Most addicts and alcoholics will concede the point and say, yes, they are willing to be willing. But not all of them.

In that case, you go nuclear. "Would you be willing to be willing to be willing to give up the resentment?" the sponsor asks cagily. Now the sponsee is up against it. She doesn't want to look like she's working a bad program. At the same time, she's really angry, but she might just be willing to be willing to be willing.

Drop the rock.

FEBRUARY 9
I'll Never Forget My First Blackout

It took place at a taverna on the Greek island of Corfu way back in 1978. I was a backpacking twenty-year-old and had planned a party for the other guests. I don't remember the party. I do remember coming to the next morning. The owner of the taverna, and his teenage daughter, were looking at me like I was the worst guy in the world. I can only imagine what I did, or tried to do.

My next blackout came a couple of months later. I was back at college, got drunk with a buddy, and passed out in my dorm room. When I woke up, the room smelled like vomit. I asked myself, "What kind of person would come into my room and throw up?"

I had no time to change to get to my campus job, so I wore the same clothing I had worn the night before. I could barely keep my eyes open at work, but eventually I realized that someone had thrown up there, too.

And that's when I realized that I had thrown up on my pants.

Not all alcoholics have blackouts,
but non-alcoholics don't have blackouts.

FEBRUARY 10
I Didn't Get in Trouble Every Time I Drank...

...*b*ut I had been drinking every time I got in trouble.

The good thing about Russian Roulette is that five out of six times, you survive. But that sixth time?

It's the same thing with drinking and driving, drinking and being around people, drinking and anything. You get away with it most of the time, but it's that one time when you don't that causes you, and sometimes those around you, to pay a steep price.

The trouble with getting away with things sometimes is that you end up thinking you'll get away with things every time. With alcohol and drugs, that's just not true. *The Big Book* calls alcohol a "rapacious creditor." You can look it up, but I'll save you the trouble. It means that you may not pay a price today, but you certainly will tomorrow. Or the day after tomorrow.

Had enough?

FEBRUARY 11
The Ballad of Tina Turner

If you're a music fan, you must know the name Tina Turner, one of the greatest singers of the last half-century. You may not know that her husband, Ike, was physically violent toward her. Once news of his abuse hit the headlines, their careers were toast.

Tina left him and went back to playing the tiny clubs she had played decades earlier, for eight years. It took eight long years before she got a recording contract as a solo artist. The amount of the deal: $8 million. The great motivator, Tony Robbins, tells that story and asks, "Don't you think Tina Turner would have rather gotten a million dollars a year for eight years than one lump sum?"

In other words, she persisted even though there was no proof that she would ever succeed again. And she did so for eight long years. The good news is that you will experience the many benefits of being clean and sober long before eight years elapse.

Alexa, play some Tina Turner.

FEBRUARY 12
Wrap Your Day around A.A.

Amazing how "busy" I was when I first came into the program. I didn't have time for the Steps, sponsorship, or meetings. I was too busy. I was also broke, unemployed, and not exactly relationship material. So what exactly was keeping me so busy?

I finally realized that I better use this time to build a solid foundation for my sobriety. I ended up going to nine meetings a week for two years. One of the things I heard back then was to "wrap my day around A.A." In other words, first, figure out what meeting I was going to, and then put everything else on my schedule, such as it was, around that meeting.

Twenty-seven years later, I still do the same thing. I wrap my day around A.A. First I figure out what meeting I'm going to, and then everything else—family, work, the gym—falls into place after I take my meeting. It's a smart way to ensure your sobriety.

First things first.

FEBRUARY 13
The Difference between Your Will and God's Will

Many of us get to the 3rd Step, where it talks about inviting God's will into our lives and get confused over how exactly to tell the difference between their will and the will of their Higher Power. The answer is pain. If you've chosen a course of action that brings pain to you or another person, that's probably not God's will. We may not know much about God, but that much seems to make sense.

The only exception to this rule is the act of getting clean and sober itself. It's painful. It's not a punishment; it's just your body going through whatever withdrawal it must face as you shake, rattle, and roll your way through sobriety.

As my sponsor, Milton, would say, "If you can make it through the day without hurting anybody, you had a good day."

First, do no harm.

FEBRUARY 14
Boy Meets Girl on A.A. Campus

That's the charming phrase Bill uses in the *12 and 12* when talking about relationships that start in mixed meetings. I don't think he was referring to today's hook-up culture.

All too many of us use 12-Step meetings as happy hunting grounds to find Mr. or Ms. Right, or more accurately, Mr. or Ms. Right Now. It's generally a bad deal for both parties. Typically, neither individual is mature enough to hang in a mature adult relationship, and most of the time, that's not what the parties are looking for. So when the whole thing crashes to the ground, as it inevitably does, now you're faced with either never coming back to your home group or sitting uncomfortably a few seats away from the person you dumped (or the person who dumped you).

You don't need to use 12-Step meetings as an opportunity to increase your dating pool. That's why God created Tinder.

Happy Valentine's Day.

FEBRUARY 15
Making Amends? *You* Don't Go on the Top of the List

Typically, when people in 12-Step recovery reach the 8th Step and start making their amends lists, they put their names at the top of the list. After all, who have we hurt more than ourselves, with all the drugs, drinking, and other antics? But my sponsor Milton used to say that alcoholics and addicts have been putting themselves at the top of the list for far too long.

Now's the time to start thinking about other people and giving them priority. So just this once, as you make your amends list, put your name at the bottom, not the top. How are we to know exactly how much pain you've caused other people? In any event, the list is not about ranking the people we've hurt in order of the amount of pain we've caused. Everybody goes somewhere on the list.

It's lonely at the bottom, but that's fine.

FEBRUARY 16
Nobody Cares about Your Cat, Your Boss, or Your Girlfriend

*C*ontrary to popular assumptions, newcomers to 12-Step recovery really couldn't care less about your "issues"—your relationship, your job, your roommate, or your parents.

Twelve-Step meetings are not free group therapy. They're a classroom, for those of us with time to guide those who are new in what it means to live clean and sober. What could possibly be more selfish than talking about our own trivial issues when the newcomers are literally dying to hear something useful?

When you share, keep in mind that the newcomer may only be paying attention for a few minutes in the meeting, and that he or she may be paying attention to you. That means that, like it or not, fair or unfair, all of 12-Step recovery may be judged on the quality of what you have to say.

Make your words count, because that newcomer
may never come back.

FEBRUARY 17
"My Goodbye Is in My Hello."

Once in an Al-Anon meeting in Manhattan, a man twenty years older than I am came over to me and said, "Shake my hand." So I shook his hand.

"Did you feel it?" he asked. "Did I feel what?" I replied, getting a little nervous.

"My goodbye," he explained. "My goodbye is in my hello. When I'm meeting you, if I want to date you, I'm immediately thinking about how I'm going to dump you."

That gentleman is speaking for an awfully large percentage of people in 12-Step recovery. In theory, we want to find the one true love that will last forever. In reality, we're just looking for someone with whom we can spend anywhere from one weekend to two years together and then dispose of in a societally acceptable manner.

If you're loving things and using people, you may not quite have the emotional sobriety you desire. If, on the other hand, you're loving people and using things, you may just be on the right track.

Don't call it love.

FEBRUARY 18
Secret Step 0

At Starbucks and In-N-Out, the cognoscenti order special items not listed on the posted menu. Similarly, in 12-Step land, only a few people know of Secret Step 0, which precedes all of the other 12 Steps.

Here it is. Secret Step 0 is "I'm tired of this $#!&."

That's right—before you even get to Step 1, you first have to come to a point where you're just sick of how you're living. Until you're able to say, "I'm tired of this $#!&," you really haven't taken the Secret Step 0. You're probably asking yourself why no one has ever shared the existence or meaning of Secret Step 0 with you prior to this moment. It's because…it's a secret!

Of course, if everybody knew it,
it wouldn't be a secret.

FEBRUARY 19
Relapse Is Optional

I relapsed eight times in a twenty-five-month period. I'd make it eight months, three months, forty days, or whatever, and then I would pick up again and be off and running.

Don't be like me.

Relapse is optional. You don't have to make it part of your story. And just because you've gone out for one day or two days or three days in the past doesn't mean you won't go out for two years or just simply go to prison or die this time around. I'm not trying to be Debbie Downer. I'm just trying to tell you the truth.

The good news, as my friend, Jerry D., says, is that you never have to drink again, if you don't want to, and you never have to be alone again, if you don't want to. All you have to do is a few simple things and relapse does not have to be a part of your story.

It's easier to stay stopped than to stop all over again.

FEBRUARY 20
It's Not an 11½ Step Program

*O*ne time I called a guy I met in a meeting and he asked me if I had meditated that day.

"Not really," I admitted. He pounced. "Then you're only working an 11½ Step program!" he gleefully exclaimed. Never called *him* again.

The 11th Step says that we sought God's will for us through prayer and meditation. This is a Step everybody reads about, but unfortunately, most people misunderstand. That's because when we say meditation today, we think of Eastern meditation, transcendental meditation, or any other practice where you empty your thoughts, breathe, and so on.

When the initial 12-Step program, Alcoholics Anonymous, was founded back in the 1930s, what its founders called meditation is today what we might call *contemplation*—just thinking about God, and listening to guidance from God.

Back then, A.A. members believed that God was actually speaking directly to them, providing guidance that they needed to check with others, to make sure it was legitimate, and then to follow. So when the Step refers to "meditating," it actually means growing silent and allowing God to speak to us and through us.

Listen to your Higher Power, why don'tcha?

FEBRUARY 21
Your Brain Cannot Fix Your Brain

When I was new, I heard a speaker at the Marina Center in West Los Angeles give the best definition of the 3rd Step that I've ever heard. He had gone to the library and photocopied a picture of the human brain from the encyclopedia.

"This is my brain," he said, holding up the photocopy. "My brain cannot fix my brain. I must take it back to the original manufacturer."

That's exactly right. The brain cannot fix itself. It needs to be taken back to the original manufacturer.

If you haven't expired, neither has your warranty.

FEBRUARY 22
God Does Not Get An Amend

The key to determining whether we owe an amend is to look at the specific language of the 9th Step. The operative word is "harm." We only make amends to the people or institutions to whom we actually caused harm.

You cannot actually harm God. You're too small and your Higher Power is too big. So the good news is that you have one fewer amend to make than you thought—you don't have to apologize to God. You can commit to behaving better, but you don't need to apologize to your HP.

By contrast, my first Al-Anon sponsor, Harv, had me write myself an amend letter, and then he had me read it aloud to him over the phone. I broke down in tears. It shouldn't be a surprise; I cry at insurance commercials. But still.

The short of it is that while you deserve an amend from yourself, God doesn't need one. If anything, you getting clean and sober is enough of an amend to your Higher Power, if one in fact needed to be made.

If you don't think your Higher Power
can forgive you, then borrow mine.

FEBRUARY 23
Who Knows More about God Than You Do?

My second A.A. sponsor, Charlie M., asked me that question when we were talking about my kids. My immediate response was to say that lots of people know more about God than I do—think about all the priests, rabbis, ministers, and imams out there who have studied their faiths.

Now, some human beings may be better educated than others about religion, but no one knows more about God than any other person. This means that you and I are equally qualified to offer a description of God as anyone else on the planet.

In fact, there are only two things you really need to know about God—one is that there is a God, and the other is that you're not it.

"Came to believe"…over time. What's the rush?

FEBRUARY 24
Why Is the 4th Step the Graveyard of Sobriety?

*P*ity the newcomer. After having been made to write all kinds of unnecessary essays on the first few Steps, he now arrives at Step 4, which has turned into the biggest production number this side of Broadway. When the program began in the 1930s, the sponsor did the writing, the process took maybe half an hour, and the goal was to list the "grosser handicaps" or the major character defects of the sponsee. That was it. It wasn't a deep dive into every bad thing the sponsees have done since early childhood.

Today, sponsors tell their sponsees to write lengthy essays about everything from childhood memories to their sex lives. As Joe and Charlie on "*The Big Book* Comes Alive" say, 95% of what's in those essays has nothing to do with alcoholism and addiction.

I believe in simplicity. Do that simple thirty minutes "back to basics" style 4th Step. You can always go back and write lengthy essays about the past later on. But for now, let's just stop the bleeding.

Overcomplicate the Steps; bury the newcomer.

FEBRUARY 25
A Balanced Addict
Has a Chip on Both Shoulders

When I was new, I was told, *pray for balance*. And my life has been in rough balance ever since. Balance means taking care of family, work, exercise, and of course meetings and other 12-Step responsibilities, without any one item dominating the rest or being left off the list.

Addicts and alcoholics tend to lead unbalanced lives. We throw ourselves into work as if the money we make will fix us. (Spoiler alert: It won't.) We then work so hard that we neglect our health, our loved ones, and the program, too.

They say that a balanced alcoholic or addict is one with a chip on both shoulders. But a truly balanced person in recovery is one who is able to find harmony among the various aspects of his or her life.

Pray for balance.

FEBRUARY 26
Can Strangers in Folding Chairs in Church Basements Really Save My Life?

*P*art of the appeal for me about Alcoholics Anonymous is the low-rent, less-than-elegant approach to meetings. On rare occasions, you're in a five-star locale, like the Women's Club in Pacific Palisades, California, or Boston's Park Street Church. Most of the time, however, you're sitting in often dingy basement rooms that don't necessarily inspire the newcomer to say, "This is the answer!"

It's only when people start talking and telling the truth about themselves, and sharing experiences, strength, and hope, and generally giving the newcomer the sense that sobriety, serenity, and a new life are possible, do they begin to get excited.

But don't let the lack of fancy clothes, or the fact that some of our best meeting rooms need a coat of paint fool you. Everything that you're looking for is right here.

For a buck in the collection plate,
you were expecting maybe the Ritz-Carlton?

FEBRUARY 27
Can You Be Restored to Sanity If You Were Never Sane in the First Place?

When I got to the 2nd Step and saw the language about being "restored to sanity," I felt insulted and puzzled. Who are these long-dead authors of the Steps to tell me that I wasn't sane? They never met me! How could they know anything about me!

But on further review, I had to acknowledge that they were right. What was sane about the way I was living? No thought of the future, no ability to hold a job. All I cared about was finding the next girlfriend and reducing my credit card debt without actually working. Anything sane about that?

I used to tell myself that everything was fine, that I was "walking between the raindrops." The only problem was I didn't realize I was drenched.

So if you're like me, and you felt puzzled and insulted by the language regarding "being restored to sanity," take an honest look back at the life choices you made while drinking or using. Anything sane there?

We think not.

FEBRUARY 28
The "Grosser Handicap" Isn't a Golf Tournament

The Big Book specifies that in the 4th Step, we simply enumerate our "grosser handicaps"—the behaviors or beliefs that block us from the "sunlight of the spirit" and keep us from growing to recovery. And yet, today, the 4th Step has turned into a series of biographical essays, turnarounds, and who knows what that were never intended by the people who founded the program.

This might not matter, except for the fact that A.A.'s success rate is under 5% today, compared to the 50% or 75% documented success rate it enjoyed in its earliest days, when the 4th Step took half an hour and not one hundred pages.

The founders of Alcoholics Anonymous never intended the 4th Step to be an exhausting roundup of everything you ever did wrong. The operative phrase: *grosser handicaps*. So if your sponsor demands that you write a series of essays when you reach that 4th Step, ask your sponsor for a source somewhere in *The Big Book* justifying the request. And if your sponsor can't find it, maybe you need a different sponsor.

The 4th Step was meant to reveal grosser handicaps;
not to be a grosser handicap.

MARCH 1
As Only the Dying Can

When I was new in recovery, I became a volunteer at a large hospital in West Los Angeles. I wasn't doing it for altruistic reasons; my goal was to meet nurses, because I had developed the idea that nurses were hot. Turned out nurses were also busy, and they didn't have time for the likes of me. But I did learn something interesting in the training program that tallied with something I had read in *The Big Book of Alcoholics Anonymous*.

As a person dies, the very last sense that remains is hearing. In other words, if we were to be dealing with a patient in his final hours, we should keep talking to him, because although they might not be able to respond, they could likely still hear us. Which reminded me of *The Big Book* line about how we "listen as only the dying can."

How do the dying listen? I can't say for sure, but I can tell you that when all you can do is listen, that's all you have. This made me think about the quality of my program. When I was sitting in meetings, was I listening as only the dying can?

Focus.

MARCH 2
No, You Can't Make Amends by Text

*O*bviously, texting did not exist back in the 1930s when the A.A. program was created. But the only evidence we have directly from the Steps about how to perform an amend suggests that Bill W. and Dr. Bob would never have turned to texting.

The key word in Step 9 is "direct," as in "made direct amends." Direct means, ideally, face-to-face. Secondarily, a phone call. But that's about it. Once we get into other forms of technologically driven communication, like texting or emailing, we'd have to ask whether we are really following the rules of the game.

How heartfelt can a text really be? "Sry 4 screwing up ur life"? And which emojis would you use in a text like that?

Apologizing in this manner suggests that we don't even care enough to pick up the phone. Doesn't that just add salt to the wound? The face-to-face amends I made were the most powerful, both for me and for the person I had harmed. Don't let our modern overreliance on technology keep you from the full benefit of the 9th Step, and don't let it keep the recipient from the level of closure that he or she deserves.

Look them right in the eye.

MARCH 3
What Exactly Is a "Whoopee Party," and Can I Go to One?

A whoopee party—who knows? It's an example of the archaic language of *The Big Book* that sometimes turns off the newcomer. Although in this case, it sure sounds like fun. Everybody's drinking, the music is loud and fast, people might just be yelling "Whoopee!" at various intervals—what's not to like?

Although we may not have specific documentary evidence of what went on in whoopee parties, one thing is certain—we can't go. *The Big Book* talks about the fact that it makes no sense to hang around people who are drinking and glumly bemoan our sobriety. As we've discussed elsewhere, those folks will get us drunk before we can get them sober.

The Big Book is also clear, however, that we need not avoid a place where alcohol is served just because we are sober—if we have a good reason for being there. Bill gives the example of a sober political candidate (there's an oxymoron!) who needed to go campaign in social settings where alcohol was in abundance. He made it through just fine. So the test is not, will I have fun? The test is, is there a legitimate reason for me being in a place where alcohol and good times are flowing?

Check your motives, and you won't get drunk or high "accidentally on purpose."

MARCH 4
It's a Bird! It's a Plane!
No, It's A.A.!

When I was three years sober, I attended the International Convention in San Diego, where a speaker from Phoenix talked about making 12-Step calls back in the 1940s. The speaker explained that they took out a small ad in the Phoenix newspaper, something along the lines of "Have a Drinking Problem? Contact Alcoholics Anonymous," with a P.O. Box.

The speaker explained that some drunk guy would see the ad and send in a penny postcard asking for help. If his address was on the card, the speaker, who owned a four-seater plane, would grab a couple of his fellow A.A.s, fly to where the newcomer lived, and since cars were a relative rarity back then, simply land on the street in front of his house.

"Imagine what that was like for the newcomer," the speaker chuckled. "You're sitting there drinking, you don't even remember sending in the postcard, and a plane full of sober alcoholics drops out of the sky in front of your home! It would be enough to make anybody get sober!"

Happy landings.

MARCH 5
Why Are 12-Step Programs like Alcoholic Homes?

Twelve-Step programs are like alcoholic homes because "there are no rules, but just don't break any." You have to be around your program for a while before you realize how and when you're allowed to speak, what sort of things are appropriate to say, and where the lines are. Twelve-Step programs also have a lot of jargon, unfortunately, that make no sense to newcomers, and that can be off-putting.

It also looks and sounds pretty strange when a room full of people in folding chairs say, often in a mechanical tone, "Hi, Fred," after Fred introduces himself, not to mention the business about repeating phrases like "could and would if He were sought," saying "Here, here," holding hands, elaborate chip rituals, and the rest of it. The newcomer may ask, "Have I stumbled into recovery or a roomful of robots?"

If you're new, remember that we all had our first day in Alcoholics Anonymous or whatever your 12-Step program might be. Some of us, like me, had multiple first days. Hang in there. Before long, it will all make sense. And so, for the first time, will your life.

Rules were made to be broken.

MARCH 6
You Can't Get an A in A.A., but You Can Get an F

Alcoholics and addicts are lazy perfectionists. We want everything to be "just right"—but we typically cannot muster the energy and resolve to make them that way. We live in a state of perpetual disharmony with people, our environment, and ourselves, because we want things to be perfect, but we just can't get around to making them perfect.

The good news is you cannot get an A in A.A., in N.A., in M.A., or in any program ending with "A." We don't give out prizes for "Best 4th Step" or "Most Courageous Amend." Although it might be fun—we could have a big fundraising gala at a big Midtown Manhattan hotel with national television coverage and give out awards for "Best Sponsor" or "Most Rehabs." And we could call the awards the Alkies.

Of course, while you can't get an A, you can certainly get an F—just by picking up or going back to the substance or behavior that got you here. You're always welcome to come back and try it again, but sometimes our ego, prison walls, or even our demise keep us from that second chance.

Twelve-Step recovery…it's pass/fail,
and the final is open book.

MARCH 7
What If I Need Multiple Programs?

You're not alone. Addiction is like whack-a-mole—you take care of your alcoholism, and suddenly you're binging on food or sex or debt or some other behavior or substance. Fortunately, there are hundreds of 12-Step programs dealing with everything from sex to smoking (or smoking during sex).

Don't be afraid to try another fellowship if a particular issue is interfering with your serenity. We didn't get clean and sober to be miserable. We also didn't clean up our lives in one area only to remain a hot mess in another. The only challenge is the question of multiple sponsors. If we have multiple programs, we most likely have multiple sponsors, which allows us to "sponsor shop," which is less than ideal.

As I worked my way through multiple programs, I always made sure that my primary sponsor in my primary program, A.A., had full vision into everything that was going on in my life. I would recommend the same for anyone going the multiple program route.

*The Big Book tells us to seek outside help when appropriate—
why not in other 12-Step programs?*

70

MARCH 8
Good Ole Rule 62

There's that old joke about the joke-tellers' convention, where the comedians know all the material so well that all they have to do is call out a number and the room breaks out in laughter. And the newcomer yells out "seventeen" and it's crickets.

"What went wrong?" he asked, embarrassed by his failure to get laughs.

"It's your delivery," he was advised.

I think of that story whenever one 12 Stepper knowingly tells another, "Rule 62," as if the newcomer had any idea of what that meant. Rule 62? Are there at least 62 rules I have to memorize to stay clean and sober? Or is Rule 62 a routine from an old Bowery Boys movie?

The short answer is that Bill, writing in the *12 and 12*, tells of an A.A. clubhouse that had actually drafted 61 rules with its members. Finally, somebody pointed out that having all these rules was contrary to the spirit of Alcoholics Anonymous. So they replaced the 61 rules with just one piece of guidance—Rule 62, which was, in its entirety, "Don't take yourself too seriously."

Why is it that we who hate to follow rules...
love to make rules for other people?

MARCH 9
You Are Not a Harvard-Trained Psychopharmacologist (Unless You Actually Are)

It bothers me that people who could barely zip up their own fly eighteen months ago suddenly believe that they have been transformed into Harvard trained psycho-pharmacologists, ready, willing, and able to dispense advice about medications to newcomers and others in the rooms.

Sometimes some of these presumably well-meaning folks will tell you, with a doughnut in one hand, a cup of coffee in the other, and a pack of Marlboros in their shirt pockets, "I don't take anything that affects me from the neck up." These are the folks who are telling newcomers that if they don't go off their meds, whether their meds are antidepressants, an antipsychotic medication, or what have you, that they aren't working an honest program.

If you aren't a Harvard trained psychopharmacologist, you have absolutely no business telling other people what to do about their medications. That's a matter for those individuals, their doctors, and perhaps their sponsors—but not for you.

Mind your own business.

MARCH 10
Whatever You Think about the Most Is Your Higher Power

*H*ow do you know who or what has the most power over you? It's the thing that you think about, obsess about, live in fear about, or generally can't get out of your head. Maybe it's another person. Maybe it's money. Maybe it's your career. Maybe it's sex, drugs, or rock 'n' roll. But whatever it is, shake hands with your current Higher Power.

One of the challenges of being human is to direct our attention to ideas or topics that are actually beneficial for us. This is especially difficult for addicts and alcoholics, who tend to remain in a state of resentment for past problems or fear over future concerns. That way, we get to avoid living in the moment, which is so uncomfortable that we have to drink or use so as not to be present to how we really feel.

So what's the solution? Identify what your current Higher Power is. Maybe it's something I mentioned above, or maybe it's something else. And then make a commitment that any time you start thinking about that person, place, thing, substance, or behavior, you'll just shake your head and say, "Next," and then start thinking about your real Higher Power.

If you don't interrupt your own thoughts, no one else can.

What if you made your Higher Power your Higher Power?

MARCH 11
"Fat, Drunk, and Stupid Is No Way to Go through Life, Son."

Who can forget those immortal words of Dean Wormer to Kent "Flounder" Dorfman, as played by Stephen Furst in the film *Animal House?*

The line encapsulates all the well-meaning advice that I received in my drinking days. It probably correlates with the guidance people share with you, sometimes in a well-meaning manner, sometimes in a state of deep exasperation, and sometimes just before they boot you out of their lives.

The last thing an addict or alcoholic wants to hear is wisdom. What we really want is simply to be left alone. But fat, drunk, stupid, and alone is no way to go through life, either. One great thing about the program is that it makes the unteachable (you and me) teachable.

It's time to graduate from *Animal House* and get on with our lives.

Time to get off double secret probation.

MARCH 12
If You Kill Yourself, You're Killing the Wrong Person

I'm not advocating homicide instead of suicide, but I have heard in the rooms more than once, "If you go from suicidal to homicidal, you're getting better." Suicide, of course, is no laughing matter. It's something that alcoholics and addicts contemplate to a much greater degree than "civilians"—and some of us, alas, follow through on the urge.

One thing that differentiates alcoholics and addicts from most other people is that we often know exactly how we would kill ourselves—we have an exit strategy. If you're debating whether you're an alcoholic or addict, and you know how you would kill yourself if things came to that, you're almost certainly one of us.

One time, I was talking with a sponsee about this. He said that he would just shoot himself in the head. I told him that sounded so messy. He asked me what I would do. I told him I would just drive into a tree at high speed on the highway. He said, "Oh, that sounds so painful." It's an absurd conversation, for anyone but addicts and alcoholics.

As my sponsor Milton used to say: "Why do people scream when they've jumped off bridges and the tops of buildings? Because they've changed their minds."

Don't take a long-term solution to a short-term problem.

MARCH 13
Bill Rode a Harley

Prior to getting sober, A.A.'s co-founder Bill W. became Wall Street's first financial analyst. He and his wife, Lois, who was also up for adventure, packed a series of stock manuals into a Harley Davidson motorcycle with sidecar and traveled around the Eastern seaboard of the United States. Bill would hang out in bars and talk to workers, getting the skinny on what was really going on inside various publicly traded corporations. He would create reports about what he learned and send that intelligence back to his comrades on Wall Street.

It's a charming, romantic episode in the lives of one of our co-founders and his ever-adventurous wife—you can find her diaries online. The only problem, of course, is alcoholism. The more Bill drank, the more his failure as a stock analyst, or as anything else, was guaranteed. Of course, Wall Street's loss was our gain. If Bill had not allowed his drinking to interfere with his life, there might never have been an A.A.

Addiction's a bad investment.

MARCH 14
Nobody Prays to a Doorknob

It's an old time A.A. cliché—that you can even choose a doorknob to be your Higher Power if you aren't comfortable with the idea of God. But I have never met a single person in any 12-Step fellowship who made a doorknob his or her Higher Power.

Twelve-Step fellowships are the only spiritual practice of which I am aware, in the history of mankind, in which members are not just allowed but encouraged to come up with their own concept of a Higher Power.

Pretty much every religion offers its own definition of God, and woe to the person who strays from that definition. Not A.A. This was the liberating message that Ebby T. brought Bill W. on that fateful day in late 1933. That's when Ebby planted the seed of sobriety that sprouted into Alcoholics Anonymous and the rest of the 12-Step fellowships. You can choose your own concept of God. How refreshing!

A doorknob opens one door;
your Higher Power opens every door.

MARCH 15
A Prayer for the Newcomer

*I*n 12-Step recovery, we define prayer as "talking to God." But what exactly do you say to God? When I was in my first year of sobriety, I had no idea. That year, I learned two things to say to my Higher Power.

First, I was told to hit my knees and then say, "If you're up there…" and then say whatever I wanted to say, acting as if a loving Higher Power was listening. It felt awkward at first, but I got used to it. Now I believe that God isn't just up there—He (or She or It) is inside me. As a result, I'm comfortable praying or talking to God.

The second prayer: "Teach me to see me the way you see me." How do we see ourselves? Typically, when we are new, as a collection of faults, character defects, bad habits, failures, and lost opportunities.

How does God see us? The way we really are—as His beautiful children. Wouldn't it be nice if your Higher Power could teach you to see yourself the way He sees you?

Say anything.

MARCH 16
Addiction: It's Fun Until It Isn't

Sometimes you can see a newcomer either at the podium or speaking from his or her seat, trying really hard to sound 100% negative about alcohol and drugs. They're afraid that if they say anything positive about drinking and using, people will laugh, criticize them, or maybe even throw them out of the meeting.

In reality, alcohol and drugs worked great for some period of time for most of us—otherwise we wouldn't have stayed with them for so long. They helped us numb our feelings. They gave us confidence. They closed out the world from us, or they made it possible for us to enter social situations that otherwise would have been too terrifying or unpleasant.

And then we crossed that line, and could no longer determine how much or how often we drank or used. As the expression goes—and substitute the proper gender and substance as you see fit—"The man takes the drink. Then the drink takes the drink. And then the drink takes the man." In short, addiction—it's fun until it isn't.

You don't have to deny the good times.
You just have to give up all hope of recapturing them.

MARCH 17
Are Your Friends Circling the Bases While You're Circling the Drain?

On Friday evenings, my drinking buddies and I had a booth at the Union Oyster House in Boston. Five or six of us would park ourselves for the evening, pouring down the Budweiser and thinking that we had the world by the tail. Couples on their way out for an evening would stop by. The men would look at us longingly, because they wanted nothing more than to sit down with us and hoist a few. The women looked at us as if we were the human equivalent of a Roach Motel.

While we were sitting there drinking, those couples were getting their careers going, putting money in retirement accounts, getting married, buying houses, starting families. They were circling the bases while we were circling the drain.

Good times.

Eventually, I cut myself off from anyone who was doing well. Why not? I couldn't hang with them. So what was the point of trying to stay in contact? And that's how we begin to find our way…to lower companions. Winners stick with winners, and losers prefer losers.

If your friends are circling the drain,
shouldn't you play for another team?

MARCH 18
Honesty: The Best Policy, or Just a Pretty Good Option?

When I got to the program, I would lie even though I didn't have to. I would hear lies coming out of my mouth and then I would ask myself, "Why did I even say that? I just invented a whole story that has nothing to do with reality, and I don't even know the person I'm lying to! Why am I doing this?"

At least I could still tell the difference between reality and deception. *The Big Book* says that we cross an invisible line when we can no longer distinguish between the true and the false. So part of getting sober is getting honest—first about our disease, and then about our true nature, and then about everything else.

I did not join the program and suddenly get honest. Instead, over a period of two or three years, I gradually became less and less dishonest, until finally, telling the truth became what I did naturally. Why did I lie so much? My best guess is that I didn't want you to get to know me, because if you did, you would hate me as much as I hated myself. So lying was a tool for self-preservation. Of course, like all character defects, once I got sober, it instead became a barrier to continued spiritual growth.

Which lie did I tell?

MARCH 19
My Drug of Choice Was...More

The Big Book tells us that alcoholics and addicts are only happy when we get more than our fair share of anything. That's because deep down, we feel really ripped off by life, cheated out of a happy childhood, a good education, or what have you. And then we aren't satisfied until we can make the world repay the debt we believe it owes us.

In truth, the world owes us nothing. As bad as our life might have been, billions of people have it far worse. In my favorite country song, "Ships That Don't Come In," Joe Diffie sings:

The things we're calling heartache

Hell, they're hardly worth our time

We bitch about a dollar

When there's those without a dime

So maybe the thing to do is to move beyond the self-pity, look around, ask ourselves what we're grateful for, and then go out and earn the things we think we'd like to have, instead of demanding them, expecting them, or even stealing them.

The goal, in this case, is to move from "my drug of choice is more" to "I am enough, I have enough, and I do enough."

Enough. What a concept.

MARCH 20
The Best Definition of Addiction I Ever Heard

*A*n addict is a sensitive person in an abrasive world who needs something to take the edge off.

We are sensitive people. We have been hurt. We've been traumatized. We've gone through things that would chill the blood of most human beings. Some of these things happened to us, and some of the things we did to ourselves.

The world is abrasive. Empathy is becoming a lost art because we're staring at our devices instead of looking into each other's eyes. We need something to take the edge off because we're uncomfortable.

So life becomes a series of choices for addicts of all stripes. Are we going to take that edge off in a negative way, by acting out on our addictions? Or are we going to follow the suggestions of our programs, and do something positive, for ourselves or for anyone else?

The Talmud states that positive actions lead to more positive actions, while negative actions breed more negative choices. So it's not just what I'm doing right now. It's the question of which path my action points me toward as I take that edge off.

Choose life.

MARCH 21
"You Could Turn Your Will and Your Life Over to the Care of an Empty Room and Get Better Results."

That's what my sponsor Milton told me one day, and boy, that hurt my feelings. Who knows what I was whining to him about. Probably something to do with my marriage, my work, or my kids. It was better than the time he told me "You could overcomplicate a three car funeral." But not much better. I guess I caught him on a bad day. Twice.

I never minded him being gruff with me—I knew how much he loved all of the men he worked with.

He was telling me that the problem wasn't something "out there"—the problem was in how I was thinking about my life. I was being ungrateful, or expecting too much of a person or situation, or lacking perception, or coming up with a solution that was worse than the problem it was intended to solve. So yes, an empty room might have gotten me better results, simply because my thinking wasn't too great, either about the problem or about the solution.

For the record, I've never said anything like that to my sponsees.

MARCH 22
I Didn't Get Sober to Feel the Way I Felt in My First Year

My strongest memory of my first year sober is standing in the library, looking at the books in the section on anxiety and trying to figure out which one to check out next.

I listen carefully when the newcomers in my meetings speak. I want to be reminded of how the disease ravages the spirit and the emotions of these otherwise smart, wonderful human beings. And by contrasting my emotional state with theirs, I'm able to see the progress that I have made in recovery.

I was told it takes eight or nine months to get the alcohol out of the bone marrow after you sober up. I'll tell my sponsees to hang in there because things will get better and they'll feel better. Or I'll suggest that what they're going through is not a punishment from God for having used. Instead, they're just going through withdrawal from their drug of choice.

The good news is that if you hang in, you won't feel anxious, scared, or miserable forever. Other people will notice your progress before you do, but eventually, you'll pick up on it too. And you'll be awfully happy you stuck it out.

If things didn't get better, nobody would stay.

MARCH 23
Yes, You Just Lost Your Best Friend

*N*ewcomers are often surprised to realize they are grieving the loss of their best friend—alcohol, drugs, random sex, overeating, compulsive spending, whatever. We derived enormous comfort from the fact that we could blow up our world any time just by buying alcohol—you can have it delivered to your home today, for crying out loud—or making a call to the dealer man (and now there's an app for *that*).

Tinder and similar apps make it easier to act out sexually. You can't drive five minutes without passing a restaurant, convenience store, or gas station that can offer up all the sugar and flour you can stomach. And now you've tossed away the security of your drug of choice for an uncertain future in a 12-Step fellowship with people you only know by their first names.

Of course, I did my grieving. I truly loved alcohol. So I wasn't just giving up a substance. I was giving up my best friend, a big part of my self-image, and my major method of self-protection. So if you're new, go ahead and grieve. It's appropriate. The good news is that as long as you do what you have to do in your program, you won't have to go through this grieving process twice.

Rest in peace.

MARCH 24
We Are Interchangeable under the Skin

Not long ago, I attended a meeting with Alcoholics Anonymous at which about a dozen individuals were present. The speaker was a young man still in his teens who was two years sober and who identified as transgender. Everyone else in the room was over fifty, and everyone listened to him carefully as he spoke. I challenge you to name one other organization, entity, or social gathering in the world today where a room full of middle-aged people would listen intently to a transgender teen, empathize with him, and learn from him.

I once heard a woman say in a meeting, "If you can find the same kind of unconditional love that you get in a 12-Step meeting anywhere else on the planet, come back and tell us about it."

Twelve-Step fellowships work because under the skin, we addicts and alcoholics are interchangeable. We come from different backgrounds, different socioeconomic levels, different levels of educational attainment, but once we get into the rooms, none of that matters. All that really matters is that each person is doing the best he or she can at trying to get another day sober.

Here, everybody listens to everybody.

MARCH 25
Shake Hands with Your New Higher Power

The first time I did a 3rd Step was in Al-Anon, and Harv was my sponsor. "Tell me about your Higher Power," he said. I thought for a moment and said, "Angry. Distant. Not listening. Used to be there for me, but not on the scene anymore. Doesn't have any real regard for me."

Harv nodded. Then he said, "Now tell me about your father when he was drinking."

I felt like I had been hit in the head with a two-by-four. My father drinking—that *was* my Higher Power. "If you could create God, and I assure you that you cannot, but if you could, what would that God be like?" Harv asked. I thought for a moment. "Caring, loving, present, interested in me, there for me." "Shake hands with your new Higher Power," Harv said.

And I did. And *that* Higher Power has been *my* Higher Power ever since.

Create your own Higher Power—some assembly required.

MARCH 26
Do I Really Need a Spiritual Awakening?

If you're an alcoholic or addict, the answer is yes. The great psychologist Carl Jung once said that alcohol was a low-level quest for God. So in some sense, when you were "getting high" you were engaged in a spiritual quest, not just a way to get wasted. The problem is that such a low-level quest for God boomerangs back on us, in Bill's terminology. After a while, it just doesn't work.

The funny thing is that many alcoholics and addicts were spiritual people when they were drinking. We weren't always able to act on our values, because the overarching value of killing pain took precedence over all of our other priorities, including keeping a job, keeping a relationship, or keeping some of whatever money we managed to earn.

And then came the 12 Steps to guide us toward a healthier form of a quest for spiritual growth. This time, though, the tools are not alcohol, cocaine, or Snickers bars. They are surrender, self-examination, restitution, and carrying the message to others.

When you take these actions, your spirit reawakens. And a reawakened spirit does not find it necessary to drink.

You can become spirited without spirits.

MARCH 27
Do I Have to Talk to My Sponsor about Sex?

You don't have to talk to your sponsor about anything. It's your business. The short of it, though, is that it's awfully nice to have someone you can talk to about anything and everything.

Just before we completed my first 4th and 5th Step in A.A., my first sponsor, Hal, asked me if there was any sexual stuff that needed to be tossed into the mix. At that time, I didn't have anything to add beyond what I had written about in my resentment list, but I was grateful for the question and for the forum, had I had anything else I wanted to discuss.

Since that time, when the topic has arisen, I certainly talked about it with my various sponsors. That's the beautiful thing about the sponsor-sponsee relationship—there are no limits, other than that which exceeds the boundaries of the sponsor's experience, strength, and hope. So the short of it is that you don't have to talk about anything with your sponsor. You can just call them up and grunt at them for all I care. But isn't it nice to know that whatever the topic, you've got someone who will lend a loving ear?

If your sponsor can't handle your needs,
maybe it's time to find another sponsor.

MARCH 28
Alcoholism—The Threefold Disease

When I was new, I regularly attended the Blueberry Muffin men's group in Lynn, Massachusetts, where one of the practices was to have a member each week describe the "disease of alcoholism."

The speaker would say something like this—"The physical part is a compulsion to drink, which means that after you take the first drink, all bets are off and there's no way to predict how much more you'll drink. You may drink until you are restrained, run out of money, run out of friends, or pass out.

"The mental part is an obsession with alcohol, where you believe that you can trust alcohol more than you can trust other people. Put those two things together and they lead to a spiritual loss of values. We all got values from our parents, older siblings, religious figures, our coaches, or somebody. But we call alcohol the Great Eraser because it wipes out all those values and replaces them with just one—getting loaded and killing the pain. So that's the three-fold nature of the disease."

The disease is the disease is the disease.

MARCH 29

When Your House Is on Fire, You Don't Care about the Name of the Fireman

This is an old Russian proverb. It refers to the idea that when a country is in trouble, you don't care who the leader is, as long as he can fix the problem.

In many ways, this is also true with the disease of alcoholism and addiction. You can go to a fabulous beachfront recovery center and spend a fortune on sobriety. Or you can sit in a dingy church basement, throw a buck or two in the collection basket (or not) and get just as sober.

Just as the disease doesn't care whether you went to Yale or jail, whether you come from Park Place or a park bench, it's the same thing with recovery. However you came in, whatever path you took, it's fine. All that matters is that you're here, now, clean, and sober.

My sponsor Milton used to be amazed that he had barely finished high school and was sponsoring a nuclear physicist (not me, mind you). That's the beautiful thing about the program—it doesn't matter where your sponsor comes from. All that matters is that he or she has something you want and has the time to convey it to you. So don't get fixated on going to the "right" rehab or the most prestigious meetings—there's really no such thing.

Don't worry about the name of the fireman.
Just put out the fire.

MARCH 30
"Here's My Number; Call Me Anytime."

That's what we tell the newcomer at his or her first 12-Step meeting. And we're doing it in good conscience, telling ourselves that indeed we are "carrying the message to the sick and suffering alcoholic or addict." But let's get real. For those of us who actually take the time and trouble to give our phone numbers to newcomers, how many of those newcomers actually take the time and trouble to call us?

I once heard someone in a meeting say, "Maybe one in fifty newcomers will call you back." So obviously we recognize that this is a poor way to get newcomers into the fold. And if we know it's so unsuccessful, why do we keep doing it?

Wally P., founder of the *Back To Basics* approach to 12-Step recovery and a regular speaker at A.A., C.A., Debtors Anonymous, and Overeaters Anonymous conventions, asks the question this way: "When did we ever start asking the sick people to call the well people?" Maybe giving out our phone numbers to newcomers isn't really 12-Step work. Maybe it's just cheap grace. What we need to do is get the newcomers' phone numbers and then follow up by calling them.

You can't carry a message to someone who never calls you in the first place.

MARCH 31
We Are Not Struck Drunk

Around the time of my first anniversary, an alcoholic made the following statement at our home group:

"We are not struck drunk. I've been around a while and I've never seen anyone deeply involved in Alcoholics Anonymous, taking the Steps, getting honest with a sponsor, going to meetings, working with others, praying and meditating, and reading the literature who suddenly had a drink in his hand and he drank it. *We are not struck drunk.*"

It's been more than a quarter of a century since I heard him say those words, and I can tell you that I've never heard of such a thing, either. Sometimes my mind wanders in meetings, but when someone says that they went out and they came back, all of a sudden you'll find me sitting upright in my chair, hanging on every word. I want to understand what caused the person to go out, and then I want to hear what manifestation of the grace of God allowed them to return. Inevitably, it all starts with cutting back on meetings. No surprise there. We are not struck drunk.

Do the necessaries.

APRIL 1
The Real April Fool

An all-too-true story. April 1 fell on a Monday at my home group that day, when the leader asked for a show of hands from the newcomers, a friend of mine with seven years put his hand up. "If that's your idea of a joke," I whispered to him, unamused. "It's no joke," he whispered back. "I had never tried crack, and I just wanted to see what it was like. I'm fine. It was just a one-time thing."

I was dumbfounded. He was a very successful attorney and man about town. On the few occasions I had been invited to some of the elegant business clubs in the city, I would often run into him, because that's where he spent a lot of his time.

It was no April Fool's prank. My friend really had given into his curiosity about crack. The only problem was that it wasn't a one-time thing, and he wasn't OK. In fact, after an eight-week crack binge, his brothers had to disconnect him from his respirator.

The moral of the story is that doing your own research would just turn you into an April Fool, no matter what the month was.

I still wish he'd been joking.

APRIL 2
God or the Bowl of Peanuts

I heard this at my very first-ever Alcoholics Anonymous meeting, back in January 1990. It was an English-speaking meeting in Paris, and I was twenty-five months from getting—and staying—sober.

The speaker was one of those dry, British types who had the James Bond-ability to make anything he'd say sound important, cunning, and wise. His comment, "It's either God or the bowl of peanuts," made a lot of sense to me. Either we reach for recovery, or we reach for something to dull our senses.

It's not as though you have to choose God all the time and you can never allow yourself a few peanuts. It's just that, well, God isn't fattening, and peanuts, if you eat enough of them, are.

Not choosing God? That's nuts.

APRIL 3
The Best Definition of Addiction I've Ever Heard

Overheard at a meeting: "An alcoholic or addict is a sensitive person in an abrasive world who needs something to take the edge off."

We may come across as tough as nails, hoping to die drinkers or druggies. But we're just fronting as furiously as we can, trying to cover up the sensitivity and emotions that our alcoholic parents may have belittled and to which the world pays scant attention. And an abrasive world it is, full of what are today called micro-insults and micro-aggressions, in which random people can say and do the meanest things, often for no reason at all.

And as a result, we need something to take the edge off. Fortunately, we no longer have to get loaded and put our lives and the lives of others at risk when we feel the urge to smooth things out. Instead of getting loaded, we can make a phone call, go to a meeting, or follow the simple-but-effective advice of my beloved sponsor, Milton—just grab a sandwich and take a nap.

Take the edge off in a way
that doesn't take the wheels off.

APRIL 4
The 12 Steps Will Do Slowly for You What Booze and Drugs Did Quickly

Alcoholics and addicts drink and use to kill pain and feel relief from whatever is going on in our lives or in our minds. The challenge for us is that when we drink or do drugs, or engage in risky or dangerous behaviors, the relief comes immediately. Even the ritual behavior that actually precedes the taking of the substance or acting out has a comforting effect.

But now we've thrown away those options for finding relief outside the program. As the expression goes, one door closes and another door opens, but it's hell in the hallway. In this case, the "hallway" is the time between getting clean and sober and no longer feeling so stressed by the world that we must drink or use. It's an extremely uncomfortable period. But the good news is that it's survivable. Anyone with meaningful clean time can tell you that they just shook, rattled, and rolled, by any means necessary, until they got to the point where they felt better.

Twelve-Step programs will get you the same relief that drugs and alcohol did, without the dangerous side effects (getting sick, alienating people, losing jobs, going to prison, or dying). That's the good news. The bad news is that it's just going to take a little longer.

Hang in there.

APRIL 5
Pulling a "Geographic"? Try to Leave Yourself Behind

"I'm outta here!" is the battle cry of literally every practicing addict or alcoholic unhappy with his or her surroundings, relationship, or job. The answer to practically any problem is to throw all our stuff in the car, assuming you have a car, and drive until you get to a place where we know no one and no one knows us, and pretend we're giving ourselves a fresh start.

This behavior is so common among alcoholics and addicts that we have a term for it—"pulling a geographic." The challenge of pulling a geographic is to make the physical move without bringing our mental state along with us. Of course, that is fundamentally impossible.

Wherever you go, there you are. Or, in our case, wherever you go, you take yourself with you. So you might as well stay put, talk things out with your sponsor, try to find some sort of resolution to the situation in which you find yourself. If not, then you'll just simply recreate the same problem, or worse, somewhere else—and you won't have the same survival network that you have where you are right now.

As Groucho Marx sang, "I must be going."

APRIL 6
How Do I Know My Sponsor Won't Tell Everyone What's on My 4th Step?

It just doesn't happen. I've never heard of a single instance where a sponsor got drunk and blabbed what he heard on a 4th and 5th Step to anyone in or out of the program. It's theoretically possible, of course, but somehow, even when they get drunk, they still respect the almost sacred bond between sponsor and sponsee.

Then, it comes back to the concept of not being struck drunk. Becoming a sponsor changes us. We realize that our sobriety is so valuable that others want to tap into it. So if anything, we protect it even more.

I've got a perfectly fine memory, but I would be hard pressed to recall more than one or two resentments from all the 4th and 5th Steps I've heard in more than thirty years in Al-Anon and more than twenty-seven years in A.A. In both cases, I'm taking those secrets to the grave, not the bar.

Trust the process.

APRIL 7
If It's Your Pain, You Might as Well Enjoy It

*J*esse Itzler is a business guy who wrote a hysterically funny book about getting fit by bringing a former Navy SEAL into his Central Park West apartment to live with him and his family and to radically step up his fitness. The SEAL, an incredibly fit specimen of humanity, loved to do things like take long runs in freezing, wet weather wearing nothing but running shoes, shorts, and a singlet, and he would make Itzler do the same thing. The SEAL would explain, "This is my pain. I'm going to enjoy my pain."

It sounds masochistic, but the fact is that in life, sometimes we have to endure pain. Getting sober? Painful. Loving people? Sometimes painful. Going to work every day? Frequently painful. So as long as we're going to have pain, what are we going to do about it?

We could hate it. We could turn it into a monster. We could make it something bigger than it is. Or we could take the SEAL's advice and enjoy it. We may be experiencing pain now because we know we are going to experience greater pleasure later on when we enjoy the results of what we've accomplished. You're going to have the pain anyway. You might as well not make things worse.

No pain, no pleasure.

APRIL 8
Twenty Weeks or Twenty Years?

*D*oes time in the program matter? Sometimes you hear people in a meeting say, "Whoever woke up the earliest this morning has the most sobriety in the room." I don't really buy that, and neither did my sponsor, Milton. He used to say, "If you're going to go on a plane, would you rather the pilot had twenty weeks of experience or twenty years?"

In other words, of course time matters. It's not supposed to be something you brag about to other people. It's worth mentioning when you share, it's going to have people pay a little more attention to your message. Ultimately, time is a way of measuring the seriousness of your commitment to the program. If you've been not just clean and sober, but active in a 12-Step fellowship for a considerable period of time, that's something to be proud of, and it's something that ought to be, and is respected.

Yes, some people have "lots of years and not enough days"— they're just as egotistical and power-driving as the day they got to their first meeting. But fortunately, those people are the exceptions rather than the rule.

Time matters, so stick around.

APRIL 9
It's All About Love

know a man whose brother Fred, in his late forties, has Down syndrome. One evening, Fred's brother took him along when a bunch of the fellas went to a local bar to hoist a few. (My friend is a non-alcoholic, in case you're curious.) Suddenly, a bar fight began, and the two main protagonists were big, beefy guys. Fred was nowhere to be found.

Until suddenly there he was, with his arms wrapped around one of the combatants. If you have Down syndrome, fighting does not compute, so he had to make the argument stop, even at considerable personal risk to himself. "It's all about love," he calmly reminded the fighters. And with those words, the tension drained from the situation. The fight was over.

Isn't it remarkable how, as intelligent as we think we are, it takes an individual with Down syndrome to tell us the truth?

It's all about love.

APRIL 10
Wow, You Really Know Me!

I had been working with my then-new first A.A. sponsor, Hal, for just a couple of weeks. The topic was women, and suddenly he exploded at me. His words, which I can recite verbatim, almost twenty-seven years on: "You don't know the first thing about women! All you know about women is how to try to f*** them! Why don't you just ask one out to coffee and *listen* to her! See what makes her tick!" I was so impressed. We had only begun working together, but he really knew me! Amazing judge of character!

Later, of course, I realized that he barely knew me from a hole in the wall, and during that conversation, he might not have even remembered which one of his sponsees I was. In other words, the advice he was dispensing was accurate for pretty much all alcoholic men, not just me. But I did what Hal said, regardless of how insulted I might have been (or it may have been how well he had pegged me for what I really was). I asked a woman out for coffee, and I listened to her, just to see what made her tick.

If the shoe fits...

APRIL 11
Eat a Live Frog Every Morning

You might say, "Why would I want to do something like that?"

I used to teach writing workshops where people would bring in their short stories or novels they were working on and we would read and review them. I had one student who, by his own admission, was a raging alcoholic. I told him about my sobriety, but the timing must not have been right, and I have no idea if he ever got sober. But I've never forgotten him because of the way his novel began: "Eat a live frog each morning because then you'll never have to do anything the rest of the day nearly as hard."

The natural tendency on the part of human beings is to put off till tomorrow anything that is too difficult to have to face right away. We'd rather not think about the things we'd rather not think about. In life, of course, we get into more trouble for the things we leave undone than for the things we do. On any given day, you most likely have a live frog. You're going to have to eat it at some point during the day.

Why not right now?

APRIL 12
Two Kinds of Love

I learned in a meeting that there is a difference between conditional love and unconditional love. Conditional love means "I will love you if"—if you get these grades, if you sleep with me, if you buy me this, and so on. It's not love at all, because you're only holding up the promise of love to the other person—you aren't giving it at this time.

John Bradshaw, a speaker and authority on family dynamics, pointed out that conditional love is actually training for prostitution.

By contrast, unconditional love means, "I love you right now, and I love you just the way you are. You don't have to change. You don't have to do things differently. You're beautiful in God's eyes and you're beautiful in mine."

That's love.

Isn't it time to move from fake love to the real thing?

APRIL 13
The Newcomer Is Listening (Well, Maybe)

According to statistics from the latest National Newcomers Survey, the average newcomer in a 12-Step meeting spends time as follows: Arrives five minutes late. Spends four minutes standing by the door, debating whether actually to go in and sit down. Takes three minutes to determine where he wants to sit, with the location calculated by proximity to the nearest exit and within viewing distance of the really hot girl or guy whose attention the newcomer wants to attract. Spends four minutes checking his phone. Spends two minutes scanning the room to see if anyone he knows and likes is present. Spends two more minutes making sure no one he doesn't like, or owes money to, is present. Spends five minutes wondering where he's going to get the money to pay the rent or ask that hot girl or guy out/buy dinner/ score. Spends up to nine minutes judging or envying various speakers without listening to a word they're saying. Spends four minutes looking around the A.A. hall and deciding that the place is a dump. Spends the next five minutes reminding himself that he probably isn't an alcoholic or addict and is just overreacting to the latest string of blackouts, parole violations, or arrests. *Spends exactly three minutes listening to someone speaking.* Leaves five minutes early.

What if the newcomer is listening to you?

The newcomer can always try to get sober again in his next life.
No big deal.

APRIL 14
The Way We Are in One Thing Is the Way We Are in Everything

The way we are in one thing is the way we are in pretty much everything. If we lie at work, we probably lie to our loved ones. If we are impatient with strangers, we are probably impatient with family members. If we are vague about money, we are probably vague about time. If we have little regard for the feelings of those around us, we probably have little regard for our own feelings as well. We may not be nice, but at least we are consistent.

Fortunately, the converse is true. Once we get sober, we can become honest in all things. Respectful of others at work, at home, and in the street. Thoughtful with people we care about and people we don't know. And an all-around good person, not somebody who appears to be good when doing so would be expedient. In recovery, we get to craft a new self-image, one that is positive instead of negative, and then we get to live consummate with that positive self-concept…in all our affairs.

Leopards cannot change their spots,
but you are not a leopard.

APRIL 15
Karma Will Be Visited on Your Enemies, but Not for Your Viewing Pleasure

The legendary "Peppermint John" of San Francisco and Santa Monica Alcoholics Anonymous loved to quote a certain French aristocrat who said of one of his colleagues, "If there is a God, he will burn in Hell. If not, he had a very good career."

In fact, there is a certain amount of justice in this world. Certainly not all the time, as we all know. But when people consistently do the wrong thing, they ultimately pay a price. The guy who sped by you in traffic, scaring the heck out of you and your family? He can't drive like that forever and get away with it. The person at the office who is lying, cheating, and stealing his or her way to the top? Not exactly a strategy for maintaining long-term employment anywhere. Word gets out.

You can call it karma, just desserts, or whatever you want. But typically, what comes around goes around—just not always for your viewing pleasure.

If you wait by the river long enough,
the bodies will float by.

APRIL 16

If Standards Are Good, Double Standards Are Twice as Good

The typical practicing alcoholic or addict can get away with anything, from sleeping with the neighbor ("her husband doesn't love her the way I do"), to stealing ("they'll never miss it"), and even murder (as they say in the South, "He needed killin'.").

We spend so much time justifying our actions that we avoid the greater issue of whether what we did was right or wrong. We don't even think about that kind of thing.

When you're drinking and using, if standards are good, double standards are twice as good. Once you sober up, it's time to start doing the right thing. Maybe not every time, but eventually more and more frequently. The habit sneaks up on you.

I may be wrong, but I doubt it.

APRIL 17
So What Exactly Is the "Bondage of Self"?

The Big Book says that the self is a source of much of our troubles. So what exactly is this mysterious "self"? I see it as a clenched fist, hanging on to all the pain and misery and suffering we have ever been through. Emotional abuse from childhood? It's inside that tightly balled fist. The girl or guy who suddenly rejected us, when we thought he or she was The One? Into the fist it goes. The guy who cut us off on the highway? Into the fist.

It makes sense that people who have been hurt by others will turn around and hurt people in their world. They'll hurt them physically. They'll hurt them verbally. They'll hurt them emotionally. They'll hurt them any way they can, because when you have a clenched fist, how else can you relate to people, apart from giving them a good smack?

When we are relieved of the bondage of self, that clenched fist opens up. We begin to release the pain, the misery, the unhappy memories. We move from a world of "somebody's gotta pay" to one of "how can I help you?"

Hurt people…hurt people.
Sober people process the pain and get on with their lives.

APRIL 18
If You Can Write a Check to Solve a Problem, It's Not a Problem

They say that a fool and his money are soon parted, but just try getting in between an alcoholic or addict and his or her dollar bills. We who used to sit at the bar and share our alcohol and drugs with total strangers may often take on a different attitude toward money when we get sober. We hang on to it tenaciously, instead of recognizing that the wiser course is to get into the flow of life by getting and sending, giving and receiving.

The Big Book says that most alcoholics owe money. Of course, we don't want to pay it, because, well, we just don't. Maybe the other person will forget about it. On the other hand, maybe the other person won't. Many an alcoholic is lying in bed tossing and turning into the wee hours, not certain of how to handle a particular financial problem. I'm specifically talking about alcoholics who owe money, but have the money necessary to pay in full whatever the debts might be. If you can write a check to solve a problem, write the check. More money will come to replace what you paid out. As Deepak Chopra writes in *Creating Affluence*, "Where will the money come from? From wherever it is right now."

I've had debt and I've been debt-free, and debt-free is better.

If you can write the check, write the check.

APRIL 19
You Say You Love Me, but You Don't Even Know Me

There are two kinds of love in the world—personal and impersonal love. Personal love is what we grow up with, if we're lucky—it's how our parents treat us, it's what we feel from our siblings and grandparents, and all the other folks in our world. If we aren't so lucky, we don't know exactly what the concept means, but we know that it's out there.

Personal love is *I-love-you* kind of love—I'm committed to you, I will always be here for you, and I will never leave you. No asterisks.

By contrast, impersonal love is what we offer the newcomer, and eventually, the world at large once we get clean and sober. Impersonal love means I don't know you, but I recognize that you are a human being, and that you're probably hurting, and that maybe we have something that can ease your pain.

So, dear newcomer, don't be confused. We love you, but that doesn't mean we're going to give you money or sleep with you. It just means that...we love you, and we will be there for you for as long as you will allow us.

Love is a many splendored thing,
even when you don't get money or sex out of it.

APRIL 20
You Can Only Be What You Must Be

In America, we tell our children that they can be anything they want to be. According to Stephen Cope, in his book *The Great Work Of Your Life*, that's not true. Cope says we *cannot* be anything we want to be. Instead, we can only be what we *must* be. And the point of life is to figure out what we must be…and then be that. I would love to be a pilot, but I'm not especially detail-oriented. I would love to play Spanish classical guitar and have the ladies all flock to me, but I have no fine motor skills. Plus I'm married.

A children's book my parents read to me, and one I read to our children, is called *Take Me to the Zoo!* It tells the story of a polar bear who can do all sorts of wonderful tricks with colors. He wants to be in the zoo. But two children convince him that he really belongs in the circus, because that's where his talents will be most valued. By the end of the book, he is convinced that the circus, for him, is the place to be. Even polar bears cannot be what they want to be—they can only be what they must be.

What must you be? The good news is there's still time.

APRIL 21
There Is No "Other Guy"

Chuck C. was a wealthy Laguna Beach, California, businessman who became sober after he read the famous Jack Alexander article in *The Saturday Evening Post*. (You can find that article online and reprinted as a pamphlet by A.A. World Services.) Chuck used to lead A.A. men's retreats, and he would talk about not just the program and spirituality, but also applying A.A. ideas in one's marriage and career. About work, he said, "I have no competitors, because I'm not competing with anyone."

When people don't feel good about themselves, they have to beat the other guy, or they'll feel even worse. The only problem with beating the other guy is that some guy who could beat you just happened not to have been born. But if he had been born, you would lose. So how much lasting satisfaction can there really be in competing and winning?

Forget the other guy, because there is no other guy.

All there is, is you.

APRIL 22
Is This the Hill the Marine Wants to Die On?

*E*ven in his seventies, he was one of the toughest men I had ever met, a genuine Korean War leatherneck who feared nothing. He was also such a raging alcoholic that, when he was on the front lines in battle and no drinking alcohol was available, he would drink his shaving lotion. As tough as he was, there was only one person tougher in his world.

His wife.

When they got into fights, he used to tell our home group she would say to him, "Is this the hill the Marine wants to die on?" No, it was not the hill the Marine wanted to die on.

I think about that story whenever I get in a disagreement with my wife. I ask myself, "Is this the hill the Marine wants to die on?" I'm not a Marine, but you get the point. It's just a way of asking "How important is it?" while making myself laugh at the same time.

Semper Sober.

APRIL 23
My Higher Power Is a Co-journeying God

One of the most profound speakers I ever heard in A.A. was a man who had been repeatedly physically and sexually abused as a child. You might think a person like that could never learn to trust God. Instead, he told a rapt audience that his idea of a Higher Power was not some sort of mystical force that kept bad things from happening. Rather, his Higher Power was a "co-journeying God," a Being that was with him during even the worst, most unimaginable moments.

Before I came to A.A., in my immediate family there had been addiction, emotional abuse, divorce, and even murder. Thinking of God as a superhero who stopped the bad guys wasn't going to cut it for me. A co-journeying God, one who was with me through the worst of it—that was something I could hang my hat on.

God is with you in the fire.

APRIL 24
Every Hundred-Pounder Was Once a Twenty-Pounder

As a compulsive overeater, I'm happy to announce that I've lost one hundred and twenty pounds over the last fifteen years. The problem is that it's the same twenty pounds, six different times.

In Overeaters Anonymous, they make the point that you don't go from a healthy weight to one hundred pounds overweight overnight. Instead, there's usually a process of trying to control one's weight, followed by pitiful and incomprehensible demoralization, which leads to the gaining of vast amounts of weight.

So the easiest way to avoid being a hundred-pounder is not to be a twenty-pounder or even a ten-pounder. You didn't get clean and sober to be the fat guy or gal at your meetings, or worse, when you're getting on a plane and spilling over into the seat next to you.

My favorite diet book is one by comedian Tom Arnold, which is titled *How I Lost Five Pounds in Six Years.*

Amen to that.

It's not the two thousand calories a day.
It's the six thousand calories at night.

APRIL 25
Nobody's Too Dumb for Recovery, but Some People Are Too Smart

In 12-Step recovery, intellect is not necessarily a blessing. It's all too easy for us to talk ourselves out of the Steps. We find logical contradictions in the literature, or we find ways to exclude ourselves from the people we don't know but we already don't like. The only problem with this attitude is that we think we're being smart, but we're really being pretty stupid.

Twelve-Step recovery isn't perfect. Instead, it's only the smartest, wisest, most spiritual approach to arresting alcoholism and addiction created since man first crushed grapes. No, it wasn't invented at Harvard, nor was it initially an app developed by brainiacs in Silicon Valley. Instead, it's a distillation of thousands of years of spiritual tradition, without the divisive nature of religion, doctrine, or dogma to divide people or stand in the way.

So, Mr. or Ms. High IQ "I'm too good for this," if that's how you really feel about the 12 Steps, then go invent your own approach to recovery that millions of people will turn to.

I'll wait.

Smarter people than you have gotten clean and sober.

APRIL 26
Everyone Has Something That Makes Recovery Hard

Young people come into 12-Step meetings for the first time, look around, and say, "I really don't want to hang out with all these old people." Women come into the program and say, "It's all men." (And they don't add, hallelujah.) Or, conversely, "There aren't enough men."

African Americans come in and may see mostly white faces. Catholics see Protestants. Jews see Christians. Asian see Caucasians. I think you get the point.

For others, the stumbling block is the spirituality of the program. Others simply think they don't have the time to get clean and sober (although they certainly have enough time to screw up their lives beyond all recognition). The reason the program works is that we are interchangeable under the skin. Look beyond the appearances and you'll find people whose hearts have been hurt the same way yours was. There's room for everybody in A.A., N.A., and all the other A's. There's room for everybody...including you.

Come on in...the water's fine. The coffee varies.

APRIL 27
Why *The Shawshank Redemption* Is the Perfect Metaphor for Sobriety

*T*he Shawshank Redemption is based on a Stephen King novella telling the story of a man who goes to prison for a crime he didn't commit, who finds an ingenious way to escape his fate, needs to bring his mentor figure along the way, tunnels his way through a river of excrement, and escapes to freedom and a new life. Sounds just like sobriety, doesn't it?

The movie came out shortly after I got sober, and I thought, *that's my story!*

None of us had alcohol or drugs forced down our throats or into our systems, of course. But all we ever wanted to do was drink or use like a normal person. And then addiction turned into imprisonment, and then a day at a time, we tunneled to freedom. If you haven't seen *The Shawshank Redemption*, you're missing one of the greatest movies of all time. And one of the greatest metaphors for recovery ever captured on celluloid.

Get busy living or get busy dying.

APRIL 28
What Can We Learn from Recovery Book Titles?

*B*ill W. was one of the co-founders of Alcoholics Anonymous and the author of much of its early literature. Lois, his ever-loving wife, founded the Al-Anon family groups when she lost her temper with Bill and famously threw a shoe at him, and cried, "Damn your old meetings!" She wrote books too. If there's a conflict between what he said and what she said, I'm inclined to go with what she said.

Back in the day, Bill was drinking, and Lois was stone cold sober. And then once Bill got sober, he remained grandiose and sometimes childish, while Lois was always the adult in the room. So if you're ever wondering whose version of the truth to trust, that of an alcoholic or that of the Al-Anon in the relationship, just take a look at the titles of their respective books.

There's the book that he wrote, *As Bill Sees It*.

And she wrote *Lois Remembers*.

What's in a name?

122

APRIL 29
Everybody Loves Progress, but Everybody Hates Change

Progress! Who could be against it? Progress is exciting. It gets us new things, new status, upgrades on our iPhones. Everybody loves progress. Change, on the other hand, is depressing. Nobody likes it. Nobody wants it. Change is scary. Why? In *The Road Less Traveled*, M. Scott Peck puts it best: "All change implies loss, and loss must be mourned."

The challenge is that you don't get progress without change. You've got to be willing to give up something in order to get something better—like the rest of life, recovery does not work on a "something for nothing" basis. If change were easy, we wouldn't need courage to face it, and you wouldn't have an Al-Anon book called *The Courage to Change*, which, of course, is one of the lines of the Serenity Prayer.

So the next time you're going through some uncomfortable change, remember that you're on the road to making progress, and that just might get you through it.

"A change is gonna come."
—Sam Cooke

APRIL 30
Rent-a-Drunk

*H*ere's an idea for an app that will make somebody a gazillion dollars—maybe you. It's called Rent-A-Drunk, and the idea is simple. In every city, we maintain a fleet of socially presentable alcoholics riding around in the back of town cars, supplied with just enough alcohol so that they can maintain without turning into a sloppy drunk.

So here's how it works. If you're in Al-Anon and you still want the pleasure of messing with an alcoholic, without any long-term consequences, you go on the app. The company delivers one of those socially presentable drunks to your door. You can reason with him, talk to him about what his drinking is doing to himself and his family, talk about the health issues, or whatever you want to do. And then when you're finished, just return the alcoholic via the convenient drop slot at headquarters.

We're providing all the fun of trying to take an alcoholic and straighten him out, with none of the long-term downsides. You can even rate the alcoholic—five stars for someone who promises to go to a meeting, fewer stars if he "just won't listen."

Ready to invest?

MAY 1
Who's Poor?

*R*elative poverty is where you feel poor by comparison to those around you. Absolute poverty, by contrast, is how the "bottom billion" in the world live. These are the individuals with nothing or next to nothing, living in dire poverty in parts of Africa, Latin America, Haiti, and other places. Most of us never compare our lives with those of the bottom billion. It's not that they exist on a separate continent; they seem to exist in a separate universe.

Here in the rich world, we are constantly making comparisons to people who have more than we do, and feeling "less than" as a result. When we do so, we are experiencing relative poverty. Our world is so focused on the material that it never even occurs to us to be happy with what we have. Instead, our advertising culture tells us that we can always be happy with more, and that whatever we have is not enough, not cool enough, or not as sexy as that convertible we saw moments ago.

If you're reading these words, you have more than enough. It may not feel that way, but you have more than enough.

We really have no idea how the other half lives.

MAY 2
I Was Sad Because I Had No Shoes...

And then I met a man who had no feet. That line is supposed to induce gratitude, but as my late, beloved sponsor Milton used to say, "He has no feet, so what does he care if he doesn't have any shoes?"

In other words, it's very hard to "make" alcoholics and addicts feel emotions they don't want to feel. We ought to feel guilty for the harm we do to other people. But when we're drinking, we're so self-centered that we are the alpha and omega of our own existences.

We don't care how we're *supposed* to feel. All we care about is how we want to feel. And how we want to feel is pain-free. Floating above the world and its problems. In an alcohol or drug-induced state of euphoria. And the rest of the world can go hang.

My first Al-Anon sponsor Harv used to say there's good news and bad news about feelings in recovery. The good news is you get your feelings back. The bad news is you get your feelings back. The good news is that you will be able to act on those feelings in a positive way, instead of burying them...and potentially burying yourself.

Feelings may not be facts, but they sure are powerful.

MAY 3
Never Check Your Email at Night

*I*t's just second nature, such a default-mode thing to do—when you have nothing else occupying your mind, you naturally gravitate toward email. Bad idea to do that at night.

If there's good news, you'll be too excited to sleep, and if there's bad news, you'll be too miserable to sleep. Of course, if there's no news, you'll start wondering why everybody has forgotten about you, and then you won't be able to sleep.

My sponsor Milton used to tell us not to analyze our lives at night. The point is that at night, we're tired, we're not necessarily our best selves, and things can look bleak, much worse than they really are. So we end up…not sleeping. And an alcoholic or addict who doesn't get enough rest is a candidate for, well, all kinds of mayhem that night and the next day. So leave your email alone, leave your life alone, and unless you really get off on animosity and strife, don't check the news either.

Remember *Go, Dog, Go* from when you were a kid? Remember all the dogs lying there in their big bed? The book says, "Night is not a time for play. Night is a time for sleep. Sleep, dogs, sleep."

As the French say, the morning brings wisdom.

MAY 4
Can We Please Get Rid Of the Newcomer Chip?

I'm convinced that many people who relapsed would return to Alcoholics Anonymous or other 12-Step programs after a relapse if only they didn't have to face the embarrassment of getting a newcomer chip. Who wants to make that perp walk from the back row to the front of the room when you get a hug from somebody you've never met and the whole room looks at you like you're some sort of big loser and offers insipid encouragement along the lines of "Keep coming back"?

Of course you're going to keep coming back. Otherwise, you're going to die. You know that already.

I truly don't understand the purpose of newcomer chips. What could possibly offset the embarrassment they cause? We should be extremely careful about putting obstacles between the newcomer or the returnee and sobriety. Can someone please make me the case that his or her early sobriety was enhanced by the obligation to pick up a "surrender" chip?

Goodbye, Mr. Chip.

MAY 5
"Tourniquet A.A." Means "Stop the Bleeding"

The point of a tourniquet is to stop the bleeding and to give the accident victim a shot at survival. Same thing with the *Back to Basics* approach to 12 Steps.

Bill W. himself wrote that the first 2 Steps are "up and down propositions"—either you agree with them or you don't. If you do, you take them as Steps. You don't need to write paragraphs or essays. You don't need to do anything. All you need to do is agree. Step 3? Same thing. No essays required. All you have to do is make the decision to bring your Higher Power into your life. Step 4 in the first decade of Alcoholics Anonymous? It took half an hour, the sponsor (not the newcomer) did the writing, and there were no essays.

So when you're working with newcomers, don't make them do the writing. Just have them take the Steps as written. They can always go back and do all that writing later on, if you or they feel the need. But the main thing is to have the newcomer take all of the first 11 Steps as quickly as possible, even if it's in a basic way. This allows the spiritual awakening of Step 12 to unfold, and when it does, the newcomer will never have to drink again.

Put the pen down.

MAY 6
Beginners Meetings, Back in the Day

In the early 1940s, A.A. offered four weekly hour-long "Beginners Meetings," during which the newcomers would actually take most of the Steps. They would do their 4th or 5th Step with a newly appointed sponsor in between the second and third meetings, and they would make their amends between the 3rd and 4th. There were variations on this theme, but this was basically how the whole thing went. And then in week five, the newcomers who had just taken the Steps…would be leading the meetings.

When Alcoholics Anonymous published the *12 and 12* in 1952, the Beginners Meetings faded away, replaced by meetings to study this new piece of A.A. literature. We have a much lower success rate with newcomers today, compared with half a century ago. Is that because those Beginners Meetings disappeared?

Fortunately, Wally P., a sober member of Alcoholics Anonymous, learned about those Beginners Meetings while talking to old-timers, and then he went and recreated scripts for those early Beginners Meetings, based on archival material he found across the country. As a result of his tireless efforts, more than eight hundred thousand in various 12-Step fellowships have attended those old school Beginners Meetings and taken all 12 Steps right away.

If you stick with the basics,
you never have to go back to the basics.

MAY 7
Depression Is Something We Do

*M*aster motivator Tony Robbins teaches that depression is not something we *have*, but instead is something we *do*. Sometimes when he addresses an audience, he'll say to an audience member who says that he or she is depressed, "Tell me how you do depression?" The person will stare at Robbins, as if surprised by the strangeness of the question.

"I'm serious," Robbins says. "Show me how you do depression. How do you sit? How do you breathe? What tone of voice do you use?"

Eventually, the person gets it. How you sit and how you speak are choices you make. Your physical state drives your emotions, not the other way around. So if you choose a more powerful state—sit up straight, breathe deeply, speak in a deep voice—oops. There goes the depressed feeling.

No, it doesn't solve the underlying issues. It just puts you in a frame of mind that allows you to focus on them and get them handled.

*How do **you** do depression?*

MAY 8
But...

*D*r. Norman Vincent Peale, minister of the Marble Collegiate Church in New York City, wrote countless bestsellers about how to live happily and spiritually no matter what was going on. In one of his books, he recounts the experience of a thirty-minute session with a parishioner who sat down and gave him a fifteen-minute speech of everything that was wrong in his life. Reverend Peale listened carefully to the man, and then said just one word.

"But..."

Startled, the man thought about the one word Peale had interjected, and repeated it. "But," he began, "I think I might get a new job...and the health situation might actually be improving...and my wife really isn't as bad as I said ..." and so on until he had talked to the end of the thirty-minute session. Peale reports that the man practically leapt out of his chair with gratitude, vigorously shaking the minister's hand. "You're the smartest man I ever met! I really appreciate your advice! You really set me straight! I feel so much better!"

So the next time you're telling yourself everything that's wrong with your life, just repeat one magic word—but—to yourself, and see if it doesn't change the way you view your life.

The truth always comes after the "but."

MAY 9
Ahh Versus Oy

Rabbi Alter Tenenbaum, leader of the Chabad synagogue in Irvine, California, says that there are two kinds of behaviors in the world. One is the kind where you say "Oy" now and end up saying "Ahh" later. The other is the reverse—"Ahh" now and "Oy" later. For me, that's the dictionary definition of recovery.

Ahh and then Oy? You're doing things that bring immediate gratification, for which a price must be paid. Oy and then Ahh? Now you're doing things that don't necessarily have an immediate payoff, but the long-term benefit is huge.

So if you're contemplating an action that might produce short-term relief but bears a potentially large long-term cost, maybe you want to ask yourself Rabbi Tenenbaum's question:

Is the Ahh worth the Oy?

Be the Wizard of Ahh's.

MAY 10
Send My Best to Your Committee

Most alcoholics and addicts come into recovery with a "committee" in their heads. These are the voices that tell us we're no good, we'll never amount to anything, everything is hopeless, and we might as well just go get drunk. The suggestion often made in 12-Step meetings is to fire your committee. My late, great sponsor, Milton D., took it a step further.

"I had a committee," Milton told our home group. "They all smoked, they all drank, none of them had a job, and they spent all day long criticizing and attacking me. So I fired them all. But when I listen to you guys talk…"—and here Milton paused dramatically for effect—"*I know they all found work.*"

Isn't it time to follow Milton's example and fire your committee?

I don't even remember hiring my committee—
I must have been drinking that day.

MAY 11
Where Do You Want the Ball?

Nancy Lieberman is regarded as the greatest female basketball player of all time. I got to know her a little bit, and she told me that whenever she had a new teammate, she would always ask the same question: "Where do you want the ball?" She explained that some people liked bounce passes, some people liked chest passes, and some people liked the ball to come in high. If you just take a moment and ask your new teammates where they want the ball, you'll be able to set them up to succeed.

The lesson is applicable in so many areas of life. It only takes a moment to find out what your coworker, partner or spouse, child, new employee, or customer wants, and how they want it. And it's just as easy to throw a chest pass, bounce pass, or a high pass. So why not make it easy for people and give them what they want, so that they can succeed? And then maybe spend a moment figuring out where you like the ball, and let the people around you know, so they can set you up to win, too.

Where do __you__ want the ball?

MAY 12
What Are You Doing Later?

This isn't a come on. I don't mean what are you doing *tonight*. I mean, what are you doing *with the rest of your life*? If you're new, your focus ought to be on mastering the fundamentals of your specific 12-Step program, learning the ropes, and taking the actions necessary to ensure your sobriety. At some point, though, you'll start thinking about what you want to do with your life.

This is a question that most people, not just addicts and alcoholics, duck. Many people are afraid of both failure and success. They don't want to take a chance on doing the thing they love more than anything else, because what if they go for it and it doesn't work out? How will they feel then? Or if things do work out, maybe they don't believe they deserve the success they will get to enjoy.

So I'll repeat the question: what are you doing later?

Whatever "it" is, go for it.

MAY 13
Make a Cup of Tea

I found this unique advice in the Al-Anon *One Day At A Time* book. A British woman who had lived in London during the time of the blitz was asked how she was able to keep her sanity despite nightly aerial bombardments of the city. "I simply did what I would have normally done," she explained. "I made a cup of tea."

In other words, when you're stressed, you don't need to recite twenty-seven affirmations or go to forty-six meetings. Even though the night might not feel comfortable, do what you would normally do anyway. If you're British, you make a cup of tea.

If you're not in your happy place, you don't have to call the dealer man, drive over to the nearest dispensary, or make a beeline for the liquor aisle. Instead, there's got to be some healthy response that you can make to the challenge you're facing. And it can be as simple as making a cup of tea.

Stress happens. Freaking out is optional.

MAY 14
Why Don't We Give Out Chips for Taking the Steps?

By putting the emphasis on counting days instead of taking the Steps, we create the false impression that if you just stick around long enough, you'll somehow "get" the program. Abstinence and sobriety are not something you get—they're something you do. The chapter in *The Big Book* is called "Into Action," not "Try to Hang Around and Hope Something Good Happens."

I don't want to sound like the Grinch who stole Chipmas. I would just give out chips to celebrate people taking the Steps. So in a meeting, it might go like this:

"Did anybody take Step 1 since the last meeting? Come on up and get a chip." Followed by applause and hugs.

"Anybody take Step 2 and find a Higher Power this week? Come on up and get a chip!"

More applause and hugs. You get the point.

When people do their 4th and 5th Steps,
they should get a standing ovation.

MAY 15
If You're Planning On Long-Term Sobriety, Buy a Black Suit

In theory, no one ever has to die of alcoholism or addiction ever again. Recovery is open to all, it's free, and if a gazillion people decided tomorrow to get sober, we would find a way to accommodate them.

In reality, some folks just won't get the memo in time. They will put their right to drink and use ahead of their instinct for self-preservation. And some will pay the ultimate price. So there's every chance that some of the people you know and love in sobriety will die an unnatural death from their disease, instead of dying sober and going to "The Big Meeting in the Sky."

That's why the old-timers used to say that if you're planning on staying sober for a while, you'd better buy a black suit. Not all of the occasions you will attend with and for members of your home group will be happy times.

Don't drink and don't die.

MAY 16
What's the Deal with Redwood Trees?

*I*f you've ever visited Marin County, California, you know how wonderful it is to see a redwood forest. Astute visitors recognize how extraordinary it is that those giant, tall trees are able to stand in such close proximity from one to the other. I once learned why in an Al-Anon meeting.

The speaker said, "Redwoods have massive root systems below the surface that you can't see. Those roots intermingle beneath the ground and support each other, helping them stand so tall. In Al-Anon, it's the same thing. Our roots intermingle beneath the surface, and we help each other stand straight, too."

To stand tall, go deep.

MAY 17
"Eat Change for Breakfast."

Jack Welch, former CEO of GE, used that phrase in his memoir to describe his attitude toward business and life in general. Nothing stands still, and if you don't eat change for breakfast, change will eat you for lunch. In nature, everything is either growing or dying. Alcoholics and addicts often try hard to be the exception to that rule, clinging desperately to a life that's grown so small, out of fear that it will grow even smaller.

Psychologists tell us that the saddest thing in life is either to stay stuck at a specific place in life or to try and skip a Step. Meaning that if we either run away from growth, or try to hasten our own growth and move too quickly, we lose.

In life, sometimes we outgrow relationships, things, jobs, schools, or places. We realize we have to move on, but we fear giving up the lesser because we aren't sure we'll get anything better in exchange. Inevitably, when we find the courage to stop playing small, and we're willing to accept change into our lives, we find improvement and not just loss. Life doesn't stand still; why should we?

Everything I ever let go of had claw marks on it.

MAY 18
Better, Different, Worse, Real

In recovery, first life gets better, then it gets different, then it gets worse, then it gets real.

Typically, the last few years prior to entering a 12-Step program are marked by a slow process of unhappiness and loss. It's only when we begin to recover that time starts to speed up on us.

So don't be surprised if things get better immediately, and then they feel very different, and then you go through a few setbacks, and then everything starts to feel…real. It's just the normal progression of things for those of us in recovery. And if your own personal experience with recovery doesn't exactly match up with those four phases, just wait. It will.

Only addicts and alcoholics can be miserable
and hate change at the same time.

MAY 19
Whatever You Pay Attention to, Grows

Everybody's familiar with Dr. Paul's paragraph about acceptance on page 419 of *The Big Book* (page 449, for us cranky old-timers).

Most of us are not familiar with what follows. My sponsor, Milton, had me read the page after the famous acceptance paragraph whenever I was unhappy about something going on in my marriage. Dr. Paul writes about his wife and how he thought about her. If he focused on her shortcomings, that's all he thought about. If he focused on her good points, however, then the good points were the only things he could see.

What's true for Dr. Paul is true for all of us. Whatever we pay attention to, grows. This is true in our recovery, in our careers, in our personal lives, and even in the way we drive. Everything is either as horrible or wonderful as you decide it to be. It's up to us.

What a wonderful world this could be.

MAY 20
Can You Love the Part of You That Hates the Rest of You?

*C*hances are, there's no one on the planet who is as mean, critical, and unforgiving toward you as you are toward yourself. This is especially true if you are an addict or alcoholic or an Al-Anon; this is doubly true if you are in early recovery.

Here's an alternative to this weirdly divided sense of self, where one part of us is judging, condemning, and hating the rest of us. What if we make a conscious effort to love that part of us that hates the rest of us? After all, if there were no part of us that hated the rest of us, our self-esteem would be extremely high. But all too often, it's not.

The easiest way to stop hating yourself…
is to start loving yourself. Am I going too fast here?

MAY 21
May You Find Him Now,
Even Though God's Probably Not a "Him"

God exists in the present moment. I've long suspected that for God, there only is a present moment, and that what we consider past, present, and future unfolds as a single idea or moment in the mind of God, whatever "the mind of God" might be.

Alcoholics and addicts love to live in the past, and not just because it's cheaper. We like to feel sorry for ourselves because eventually we come to believe that we deserve the next drink, drug, or addictive behavior. Similarly, we're also very comfortable in the future, since we probably won't have the exact same set of problems we have right now. We love the future, because in the future, everything is perfect.

The work of the recovering alcoholic, addict, or Al-Anon, therefore, is to make a comfortable nest of the present moment. Why? Because the present moment is where God can be found, and if you're with your Higher Power, you don't need to act out on an addiction or compulsion.

The present moment is a gift—
that's why they call it "the present."

MAY 22
Do Your Bad Deeds in Public and Your Good Deeds in Privatee

Wait a minute—isn't it the other way around?

For most of us, yes, it is the other way around. But this piece of advice from the Talmud is definitely worthy of a second look. Most of us try to hide whatever bad acts we do from ourselves, other people, the authorities, our partner or spouse, our children, our employer, and so on. Hiding is exhausting. It's an energy suck.

By contrast, if we do something good, whether for ourselves or for someone else, we want the world to know it. In fact, extroverts are "someone to whom nothing happens until they tell someone else." You might be saying, "But I like it when people know the good things I did. I want everyone to know what a wonderful person I am."

Trust me—we already know.

You can always tell people
about your good deeds some other time.

MAY 23
How Long Will You Put Off Happy, Joyous, and Free?

*O*nly an alcoholic or addict could stand at the crossroads of insanity, institutions, and death in one direction, and happy, joyous, and free in the other…and scratch his or her chin.

In other words, we, more than most people, can make a Heaven of Hell or a Hell of Heaven, in John Milton's words, simply based on our attitude. Now that you're in recovery, at some point you'll get a sponsor and take the Steps. The sooner you do, the sooner you put yourself on the path toward being happy, joyous, and free, instead of, well, the opposite.

What are you waiting for?

"When you realize you want to spend the rest of your life with somebody, you want the rest of your life to start as soon as possible."
—*When Harry Met Sally*

MAY 24
We're Easy on Ourselves, and Hard on Everyone Else

We can only control two things in life—our words and our actions. Everything else, including our thoughts and the behavior of other people, is out of our hands. If we're going to base our happiness on how well the people around us behave, we're in for unhappy times. If, on the other hand, we're willing to be a little tough on ourselves and set high (but not impossible) standards for what we do and say, we'll be much happier.

We have to be harder on ourselves and easier on those around us. If we're too demanding and exacting of those around us, they won't stick around. Isn't it time to toughen up a little on ourselves and lighten up a little on everyone else?

We judge ourselves by our intentions,
but the world judges us by our actions.

MAY 25
Every Meeting Gets Better or Worse, One Share at a Time

Ever notice that when one person starts to complain about what's going wrong in his or her life, everyone else feels comfortable following suit? Or if one person says something funny, and the room erupts in laughter, the next person wants to make the room laugh too?

Every time we speak in a meeting, we make that meeting incrementally—or sometimes drastically—better or worse. If our message is positive, we encourage others to share the good things happening in their lives. If our message is negative, the converse happens.

And then next week, people have a sense of what the culture of the meeting is based on what happened the previous week. Some meetings have reputations for being "stitch and bitch" sessions, while other meetings have a reputation for giving you sixty minutes' worth of recovery in the sixty minutes the meeting lasts.

This is one more reason why, when we share, we strive to be useful. What we say influences ourselves at a cellular level because our subconscious believes every word we say. But we're also influencing everyone else, and we're affecting the overall quality of the meeting. So choose your words carefully.

The newcomer is listening.

MAY 26
Drop Dead? Who Cares!

In *Younger Next Year*, a book about aging, Chris Crowley tells the story of a spry eighty-year-old who still loves to clamber up the mainsail on his fishing boat.

"Aren't you afraid you're going to fall in the water and drown?" his cautious friend asks.

"Who cares?" the eighty-year-old smiles back.

Most of us spend far too much time thinking about the negative consequences that could come from a decision to "go for it" in life. Or we think about the imaginary critics who will decry us for having taken a shot at what we really wanted to do. Life's too short—actually, life's too long—to spend a moment thinking about those imaginary inner or outer critics.

The eighty-year-old on the boat knew as much. He figured, "I've had a good life. I'm going to die at some point. So what's the difference if I fall off the boat and end up in the water?" For him, real death would have been the decision to stop doing what he loved, namely, keeping his boat in tip-top shape.

Do what you love, because otherwise...
you'll be doing what you don't love.

MAY 27
What's on the Menu in Heaven and Hell?

Yet another Zig Ziglar story for you. Ol' Zig, the great motivator, used to say that in Heaven and Hell, there are long banquet tables, with oversized forks, knives, and spoons. In Hell, no one's eating, because they can't figure out how to eat with two-foot-long cutlery. In Heaven, it's a party, because they're using the implements to reach across the table and feed the people to whom they are sitting opposite.

In other words, Hell is when you aren't looking out for the other guy and he isn't looking out for you. Another way to describe that miserable state of being is "active addiction." By contrast, when everybody is looking out for each other's best interests, that's Heaven.

The food's the same, the table's the same, the forks and knives are the same, and the people are probably the same. The only difference is their attitudes.

"Go to Heaven for the climate, go to Hell for the company."
—Mark Twain

MAY 28
Who Else Can Benefit from Your Success?

Jay Abraham is the preeminent marketing genius of our times. He has consulted for thousands of companies around the world and speaks to sold-out audiences on three continents. One of the questions he teaches businesspeople to ask is this: "Who else can benefit from your success?" In other words, maybe you have a product but no marketing channel for the product. Or you've got a marketing channel and nothing to sell. So you ask yourself who's got what I don't have, and together can we make great things happen?

Isn't that the essence of recovery? If you're new and you get clean, the old-timers in your meeting notice, and it brings them more joy than you may realize right now. If you've got clean time and you carry a message to the newcomer, either face-to-face, as a sponsor, sharing from your seat in the room or sharing from the podium, you're making a huge difference in someone else's life. If one of us wins, we all win.

In 12-Step recovery, who benefits from your success? Everyone.

*Not to mention your family, your friends,
your coworkers, your pets, other drivers…*

MAY 29
The Great Unjumbler Strikes Again

The first edition of *The Big Book of Alcoholics Anomynous* contained a story in which a newcomer describes an encounter he had at his first meeting with A.A. co-founder Bill W. Can you imagine that? You go to a meeting, and the very first person you talk to is Bill? How wild is that?

The newcomer wrote, "I told Bill, 'I've made a jumble of my life.'" To which Bill replied, "Would you be willing to let God unjumble it?"

I love this story because it indicates the fact that A.A. has been a spiritual program from its inception. Bill didn't tell the person what kind of God should do it or how to pray to God, but by the same token, he also didn't advise the newcomer to go to ninety meetings in ninety days. He wasn't shy about stressing what he called A.A.'s "spiritual angle." So why are we?

You don't have to keep your HP a secret.

MAY 30
Working the Steps Backwards

My sponsor Milton used to say that when people are getting ready to drink, they stop working the Steps in the opposite order from the way they initially worked them.

First, they stop working with others in Step 12. Then they stop praying and meditating in Step 11. Then they stop being responsible for their actions and making amends in Step 10. And so on, until they have no character defects and everything is everybody else's fault, and they're their own Higher Power, and they are no longer powerless over alcohol or drugs.

And then they wait until the moment arrives when there's drugs, alcohol, or Mr. or Ms. Wrong is in the building, and they're off and running. How do they look back on their time clean and sober? If they could be honest, with deep regret for getting away from recovery. But they usually can't be honest—as *The Big Book* says, they can no longer distinguish the true from the false.

About this time, they start telling their drinking and drugging friends that "A.A. is for quitters."

Don't untake the Steps.

MAY 31
Carry the Message, Not the Addict

Sponsorship involves walking the fine line between guiding alcoholics and addicts versus picking up and carrying them. Newcomers can be awfully manipulative—after all, weren't we? Newcomers are often happiest when they can figure out ways for us sponsors to do the work. But in the long run, it doesn't do them any good if we become a nurse instead of a guide and confidant.

A sponsor is not a bank. We don't give our sponsees money, we don't lend them money, and we don't hold on to money of theirs, lest they use it to buy alcohol or drugs. We encourage them to find work, but we aren't a job fair. And we're not a lonely hearts department, dispensing relationship advice as if we were such great experts at the topic.

So what do we do? We share our experience, strength, and hope. We let them make their own mistakes and learn from them. We listen and listen and listen. Above all, we love them until they can love themselves…and then we keep on loving them.

We don't play God to our fellows.

JUNE 1
If It Doesn't Stop at Your Station, It's Probably Not Your Train

We alcoholics and addicts love to force things—we love to force solutions, we love to force people, and above all, we like to impose our will on any and every situation in which we find ourselves. Why do we do it? Because when we're in control, we feel safe, so we tend to equate getting our way not just with success but with survival.

So if you're feeling frustrated because the train you were trying to jump on didn't stop at your station—the solution you were imposing didn't apply or was simply ignored—it probably wasn't your train.

Be patient. If you stay on the platform long enough, your train will appear. The good news is that you don't have to be driving it.

Here comes the express.

JUNE 2
An Expectation Is a Preconceived Resentment

If I expect that everything is going to go perfectly well, then I'm not exactly living life on life's terms. Here on Planet Earth, there are ups and downs. Disappointments. Frustrations. Even tragedy.

I once heard in a meeting that your life may look like a series of ups and downs to you, but to your Higher Power, it looks like an arrow pointing up. The trick of life is to stop being surprised by seemingly negative events. That way, instead of having to focus on our own unmet expectations when difficult things happen, we can focus on the events themselves and see how we can make things better, for ourselves and those around us.

Stop writing scripts.

JUNE 3
Hitting the Red Brick Wall

Whenever I had an idea that was clearly not a great idea, my second Al-Anon sponsor, Jan, would always say the same thing. "If you want to hit that red brick wall, I'm not going to stop you. I'll be there to pick you up, when you're bloody and bowed after you've run full speed into that red brick wall, but I'm not going to keep you from running into it."

That was about as strong a signal as she could give me that the choice I was making was not a good one. But that's really what good sponsors do—they point out the likely outcome of a decision, good or bad, but they don't prevent the sponsee from learning the lesson that needs to be learned.

Is it painful for the sponsor to watch the sponsee run into that red brick wall? Of course it is, but we cannot adjust our sponsorship to make our lives easier. Instead, we have to do what's best for the sponsee, and often, that means allowing him or her the dignity of experiencing the results of their choices.

Nobody said you had to learn the hard way.

JUNE 4
Detachment Need Not Be Amputation

In the Al-Anon fellowship, we speak of detachment as a desired outcome of working that program. But sometimes the word "detachment" can be misunderstood. That's because there are different levels of detachment. The ideal is detachment with love, where the alcoholic in our lives has the freedom and dignity to behave as he or she sees fit, and during the consequences of that behavior, perhaps learning from those experiences.

Detachment with love doesn't come easily, and it usually doesn't come overnight—not after years or even decades of unhappy experiences, attempts to control the other person's drinking, lashing out, and the like. Sometimes the overwhelming desire to just chop the other person's head off, at least metaphorically, has nothing to do with that person.

It could be that detachment with an axe, or detachment-as-amputation is a necessary step on the road to detachment with love. So if that's where you are with the alcoholic or addict in your life, keep in mind that the goal with 12-Step recovery isn't to erase people from our lives. It's to be able to accept them for who they are and what they are, without any negative impact on our own lives.

We can always get better at detaching.

JUNE 5
How I Took Step 8

Step 8 asks us to make a list of all persons we have harmed. Sometimes, we forget or even bury the harm we do to others, or we implore the technique of "comparative negligence" and justify our bad behavior by telling ourselves that the other person's actions were worse than ours.

I didn't have that luxury. When I got to Step 8, I had one of those old school address books where you write people's names, addresses, and phone numbers in ink into the book. This was long before the advent of smartphones. Back when I was drinking, if someone annoyed me enough, I would take "white out"—the fluid typists used back in the day to cover up mistakes—and I would simply eliminate that person's name and contact information from my phone book. So when it came time to do my 8th Step, all I had to do was hold the book up to the light, page by page. Pretty much everyone I had whited out ended up on my amends list. No surprise there.

Nobody's perfect.

JUNE 6
Why Wise People Are Smarter than Prophets

Prophets are those who can see the future, so it's hard to imagine that anybody could be smarter than they are. Yet wise people have a gift that even prophets don't have—they can see the present.

Obviously you have to plan and prepare for the future, because it's coming. But along the way, are we living in the moment? Are we enjoying our lives, or just turning everything into drudgery? We addicts and alcoholics can be a little bit masochistic, and we can take the idea of delayed gratification a little *too* far.

So yes, it would be nifty to be able to see into the future, to be prophets. But I'll settle for being wise enough to see what's happening right now—in my own life, in my relationships, in my recovery.

If you keep your eyes on the present,
the future takes care of itself.

JUNE 7
We Need to Be
What We Want Others to Become

There was an off-Broadway play that ran in New York and around the country for years called "I Love You, You're Perfect, Now Change." Doesn't that sum up pretty much every relationship that every alcoholic or addict, practicing or sober, has ever entered into?

We are idealists, at least when it comes to the behavior of other people. We know what's best for them, and we're more than happy to show them how to achieve what they need to do and to be. But when it comes to our own behavior, we typically just give ourselves a pass.

What if we committed to being what we keep trying to make other people become? What if we took on the characteristics, behaviors, and attitudes that we expected to see in others? Since water finds its own level in relationships, other people are far more likely to be what we want them to be if we ourselves are that kind of person first. And if we model ourselves on our Higher Power—trying to be loving, kind, present, and listening—we can't go far wrong.

Take the microscope off ourselves
and others and put the telescope on God.

JUNE 8
Happiness Is a Victory of Intellect over Emotion

If we look around at the world around us, we can find plenty to be unhappy about. First, we're mortal and we're going to die. (Sorry to break the bad news.) Next, there is poverty, inequality, war, and all manner of bad things happening on the planet even as we speak. From an emotional standpoint, you have every reason in the world to be unhappy.

This is where the intellect comes in. This is where we put the I over the E, or the intellect over the emotions, as the old-timers used to say. Sure, the world in general, and perhaps our own corner of the world, might be imperfect, messy, and depressing at times. We can still choose to be happy.

Happiness is indeed a choice. It's a decision that we make that sometimes flies in the face of all rational evidence. When I was a kid, I always thought I'd grow up to be like Winnie the Pooh. Instead, as a practicing alcoholic, I turned out to be Eeyore. Today, I choose to be happy, and if I'm not happy, I do something about it.

"Most people are as happy as they make up their minds to be."
—Abraham Lincoln, from the Al-Anon Just For Today bookmark

JUNE 9
Your Business Is Going to Meetings...

...So anything that happens outside of a meeting is none of your business.

Alcoholics and addicts new to recovery typically live with a sense of impending doom, and often rightly so. Clancy I., founder of the Midnight Mission and the Pacific Group, says that if you stop drinking and all of your problems go away, you're probably not an addict or alcoholic. If you stop and now your problems pile up on you, you're most likely one of us.

If we stick around, those things all get handled, one by one. As *The Big Book* says, most of us owed money when we got here. Most of us either had no relationships or poor relationships. The longer you stay clean and sober, the more likely that you'll be able to tackle those issues and put them behind you.

If I get too wrapped up in my problems, I'm setting myself up for relapse. I can remind myself that other people had these same issues and got through them. That's why we shift from dwelling on our problems to studying the meeting book and figuring out which meeting we're going to next. Going to meetings is my business; everything else is none of my business.

So mind your own business.

JUNE 10
Who Cares?

This is a "mean old sponsor" trick that not even my sponsor Milton played on me. The newcomer asks a sincere, heartfelt question about a problem that is upsetting him or her, and the sponsor says that the answer can be found in the first two words of the chapter on Step 1 in the A.A. *12 and 12.*

The newcomer hunts down a copy of the book and finds the relevant page, only to discover that the first two words of the chapter on Step 1...are "Who cares."

Deep down, your sponsor cares. He's just trying to help you put things in perspective. There may be more sensitive ways to do that, however.

We kid because we care.

JUNE 11
It's Running Now

When I was newly sober, I had a 1988 Ford Taurus with a balky computer system. Sometimes it would start, sometimes not. So I took it to an auto mechanic, and he told me to go down the street to a coffee shop and give him forty-five minutes to figure out the problem. He also told me not to turn the car off. When I came back, he gave me that "mechanic shrug" indicating that he had no idea what the problem was.

"It's running now," he added helpfully.

At least he didn't charge me.

Whenever I've got some sort of issue in my life to which I can't figure out an answer, I often think of that moment. My thinking certainly has some faulty programming in it, and some mornings, I just can't get started, or I'm just not operating at full strength.

"It's running now," I'll remind myself. In other words, my life may not be running 100% smoothly, but at least it's running. Probably yours, too.

At least he didn't charge me.

JUNE 12
Dr. Bob Was Right

One of the most moving and meaningful speeches ever made by a human being is the final address of Dr. Bob at an A.A. gathering shortly before his death. "Let's not louse it all up with Freudian complexes," he told the audience, recognizing from his fifteen years of sobriety that alcoholics love to overcomplicate everything. "Our 12 Steps, when simmered down, resolve themselves into the words 'love' and 'service.' We understand what love is, and we understand what service is."

Alcoholics and addicts are seekers. The beautiful thing about the program is the simplicity and clarity it brings to some of the hardest questions in life.

We all know what love is, and we all know what service is. We don't have to overcomplicate things. Are we being of love and service? It's typically a yes or no proposition. Either we are or we are not. And if we are not, why are we being so selfish? If you're looking for a philosophy of life, try "love and service." Works like a charm.

"You could overcomplicate a three car funeral."
—*My sponsor, Milton*

JUNE 13
Pain Is Mandatory;
Suffering Is Optional

There's no such thing as a life without pain. From growing pains to the pain of loss, it's one of the fundamental experiences of life. It's not even a bad thing—we say "no pain, no gain," or as they say in Hawaii, "no rain, no rainbows." On a deeper level, *The Big Book* reminds us that pain is the touchstone of all emotional growth.

Suffering, by contrast, is not obligatory. It's strictly optional. Suffering is what happens when we have pain we don't take care of. If I get an unexpected tax bill, that's pain. If I don't respond, and the IRS attaches my bank account, I'm just creating suffering for myself. After all, they don't want *my* money—they want *their* money.

We always have a choice, once confronted with pain, either to face it or to let it fester and turn into suffering. What are you going to do with your pain—let it grow or let it go?

Pain is a teacher, not a punishment,
so pay attention to it.

JUNE 14
My Pain Is Not in the Facts;
It's in My Resistance to the Facts

It all comes back to acceptance. My sponsor, Milton used to say, "If you've got a problem and you can accept it, you don't have a problem anymore."

Acceptance doesn't mean liking a situation. It just means acknowledging the reality of whatever is going on at the moment. If I can do that, I'm in acceptance. I may flip in and out of acceptance on a given issue, because one moment I'm OK with it and the next moment I'm not. But aiming to be accepting of whatever's happening in my world—that's the goal.

Acceptance is not weak-kneed submission. It means doing everything I can to make an unfavorable situation better, instead of just lumping it. But the facts are the facts. If I'm unhappy, it's not because the facts are what they are, it's because I'm resisting the facts. I'm fighting City Hall. I'm not dealing in reality.

So my goal as a clean and sober person is to accept the facts of what's going on, and then to decide, in as cool and level-headed manner as I can muster, what, if anything, I need to do to make things better. And then I need to get busy doing those things. That's living sober.

I only need to accept the things I don't like.

JUNE 15
Let the Whirling Dervish Whirl

*O*ne aspect of the Sufi religion is to worship God through whirling at high speed. Not all Sufis do this, and some dervishes are not Sufi, but that is the group most commonly associated with the concept of the whirling dervish. Ever tried to stop a whirling dervish? Not easy to do.

But have you ever tried to influence the thinking or actions of a practicing alcoholic or addict? Have you tried to do so repeatedly, despite the fact that you're having no success whatsoever? Does it seem like your entire life is devoted to trying to get that whirling dervish—I mean that alcoholic or addict—to stop whirling?

Let them do what they need to do. They're going to do it anyway. Why not preserve your energy for something that productive?

Live and let whirl.

JUNE 16
The Merry-Go-Round of Denial

We all know what a merry-go-round is. It's where you go up, down, and around, but you don't really get anywhere at all. In the merry-go-round of alcoholism, according to Al-Anon, the alcoholic says or does something to provoke the Al-Anon. The Al-Anon, angered and hurt, lashes out at the alcoholic. Now the alcoholic has an excuse to drink, and someone on whom to blame his or her drinking. That's the merry-go-round of denial. Both parties have no idea that they're even on a merry-go-round in the first place.

So Al-Anon suggests that its members get off that merry-go-round. When those ritual provocations arise, don't respond in the usual manner. Instead, take a deep breath. Respond with a soft tone. Say something that isn't inflammatory, like, "You might be right," or "Hmm." In other words, don't engage, because if you do, the alcoholic is now free to drink and blame you.

Ever gone on a real merry-go-round all by yourself? Of course not. It's lonely. A merry-go-round is something you do with someone else. So if you're the Al-Anon and you get off the merry-go-round, the alcoholic has no one to go around with. Many times, they just quit drinking altogether because you took the fun out of it.

You can get off anytime.

JUNE 17
Stop Asking Questions That Have No Meaning

*E*very child asks the same question: Why? As in: Why do I have to go to bed? Why do I have to eat spinach? Why do I have to go to school? Why? Why? Why? Parents, depending on their attitudes, may resort to, "Because I said so," or they may offer an elaborate explanation, hoping to satisfy the curiosity of the child. Either way, the kid still has to do it.

In recovery, the word "Why" typically introduces questions that have no meaning. Why am I an alcoholic or addict? Who knows? The point is that you are one. Why does my husband keep doing or saying…whatever he keeps doing or saying? Who knows? It's just how he is.

This is your life. You're an addict or an alcoholic, or you love someone who is one of those things. The why of it doesn't matter. What's important now is what you're going to do about the situation confronting you. Will you give up? Or will you get a program, get a Higher Power, and get a life?

So stop asking questions that have no meaning. Maybe ask, "What can I do right now to make my life better, more fun, more successful, and more enjoyable?"

Why ask why?

JUNE 18
Whose Feelings Are You Feeling?

Alcoholics and addicts, like addiction itself, can be cunning, baffling, and powerful. This is true whether the alcoholic in our lives is a parent, child, sibling, or love interest. They can be so powerful that we may need to ask ourselves, when we are feeling a feeling, whose feeling is it—mine or the addict's?

There's nothing wrong with empathy, the ability to feel compassion for the pain of another person, or to feel that person's joy, for that matter. The trouble comes when I am the hostage to the emotions of the addict or alcoholic, practicing or sober, even alive or dead. I've got to ask myself, at every turn, whose feelings am I feeling?

Am I angry because he's angry? Am I envious because she's envious? Or are these my own feelings? If finding the answer to these questions seems impossible, or if the questions themselves make no sense, my suggestion would be to try out the Al-Anon fellowship. There, among other things, we learn to distinguish between our own feelings and the feelings of others, so that we can make appropriate choices with our lives by putting ourselves, not the addict or alcoholic in our lives, first.

Where you end and I begin—that's boundaries.

JUNE 19
Perfection Is Hard to Love

Perfectionism is a character defect that resonates with the lives of many, if not most, addicts and alcoholics. Perfection is also very hard to love.

In all great movies and novels, the main character has some sort of flaw that he or she has to overcome in order to reach a desired goal. To be flawed is to be human. Indeed, the word "vulnerable" comes from the Latin word *vulnus*, which means wound. When we're vulnerable, we're wound-able.

By contrast, people who appear perfect, who are always trying to say and do the perfect thing, are exhausting. They're superhuman, or at least they're trying to be, and that leaves the rest of us in the dust. Which sets up a sad, but true, reality: You can be perfect, or you can be loved.

Ironically, if being perfect has been your strategy to achieve love, it's time to find a new strategy. That's why sponsorship is such an incredibly powerful and life changing tool, because for people like us, it's often the first time that we were loved because we weren't trying to be perfect. We were trying to be real.

It's perfectly OK...to be perfectly imperfect.

JUNE 20
The Absence of Profanity Will Offend No One

That's the slogan you hear every so often in 12-Step meetings, and it's true. I remember a world where gentlemen never used inappropriate language in the presence of ladies, and ladies never used inappropriate language in the presence of men.

That's so over.

Instead, we live in a world where it's acceptable, if not exactly pleasant, for men and women to curse like sailors, even if they were never in the Navy. I don't want to be a public scold, but I will suggest that the use of profanity in a meeting indicates a certain laziness on the part of the speaker—an inability to dig deeper and find a less profane way of expressing his or her thoughts.

At the same time, believe it or not, there are people who find offensive language…offensive. Some of them may be newcomers. Is your choice of language potentially alienating the people new to the program? You can always go outside and curse during the break.

Watch your language.

JUNE 21
My Need for Recovery Outgrew My Need to Use

Alcoholics and addicts are nothing if not clever. We only do things that we are convinced will benefit us. If we're hanging around a particular person and the flow of affection, drugs, sex, money, or whatever else we're looking for dries up, we move on. We're always putting our own survival—and our ability to feed our disease—ahead of everything else in life.

At some point, though, we begin to recognize that defending our right to drink and use just isn't worth the hassle, the price, the losses, the jail time, the alienation of affection of loved ones, or whatever we hold dear. So we do a cunning calculation in our own brains. We don't recover necessarily because we want to stop drinking and using. We recover because we're tired of paying the price.

Whatever brings you to recovery, whether the motive is positive or negative—it's perfect. As long as your need for recovery outweighs your need to use, you will stay on the right path. Coming to meetings regularly is the best way to remind yourself of the benefits of what you're doing, whatever your initial motivation might have been.

We stood at the turning point.

JUNE 22
Every Time I Hear the Definition of Insanity, I Expect It to Be Different

Albert Einstein is credited in 12-Step land with the aphorism, "The definition of insanity is doing the same thing over and over and expecting different results." Einstein was wrong. For addicts and alcoholics, doing the *same* thing over and over and expecting the same results is insanity.

For proof, consider the progressive nature of addiction and alcoholism. As time goes on, you need more and more of your drug of choice to achieve the same high. So there's a situation where it's insane to expect that the same actions will get you the same results. Similarly, in relationships, people change. What you did yesterday to demonstrate your love for the other person may not be sufficient today.

So let's not get in a rut, people. Instead, let's recognize that it's insane to do the same thing over and over again and expect the same results. Life is simply too variable for that to happen.

I'm not saying I'm smarter than Einstein, but...

JUNE 23
Your Subconscious Mind Is Listening

Your subconscious mind cannot distinguish between reality and whatever you say is reality. So whatever you tell yourself, not only will you believe, but you will do everything in your power to make true. That's because human beings need to feel consistent with their words and their actions. If you tell yourself, "I just can't get the program," your subconscious mind will do everything it can to make those words come true. On the other hand, if you tell yourself, "I can do this," the reverse will be true.

If your subconscious is listening, and ready to turn your instructions, positive or negative, into reality, why not tell yourself something positive, and allow that to become true? Maybe you don't think anyone's paying attention when you speak, but your subconscious mind is hanging on your every word.

Give yourself some good news.

JUNE 24
Nobody Cares, and Besides, It's Over

When I was a kid, *Mad Magazine* used to run a feature where they would take a common expression that everybody used without thinking about and then turn it into a drawing, to illustrate how silly it is. The one I remember best is "Nursing a grudge" which depicted a "Grudge" as some sort of angry-looking, Dr. Seuss-like creature that someone had with a baby bottle filled with milk. That person was literally nursing the Grudge.

When you put it that way, doesn't that sound laughable? Of course. But isn't that something we do every day? Alcoholics and addicts don't just nurse our grudges—we love them, we caress them, and if we could have our way, we might just keep them forever.

And then comes the program to say that grudges are not exactly acceptable household pets. In fact, it's probably best if we let the grudge go and get on with our lives. How do we do this? By writing about it, talking it over with a sponsor, identifying our part in the situation, identifying the underlying character defect or bad habit in us, praying to have that removed, and then acting as if the situation and that underlying defect of character has been removed.

Move on.

JUNE 25
I'm Not Always a Happy Camper, but at Least I'm a Healthy One

Where do we get the idea that by accepting the gift of sobriety, we will be happy all day long? That's just not how recovery works, and it's not how life works. Stuff is going to happen from time to time that you aren't happy about. What's the right course of action—stress over it? Stamp your feet like Rumpelstiltskin? Run away? Or get drunk or high, or otherwise act out on a bottom line behavior?

Reality means accepting the fact that we aren't going to be happy all the time. Instead, we get to be healthy, make healthy choices, surround ourselves with healthy people, think healthy thoughts, or at least most of the time.

The promise of recovery is being relatively comfortable most of the time.

JUNE 26
You Can Tell Your Friend Your Truth Just One Time

I'll tell you exactly what Harv, my first Al-Anon sponsor, used to tell me: "You can tell your friend your truth one time, and if they get it, great. If they don't get it, you have to get that they didn't get it." In other words, we alcoholics, addicts, and Al-Anons have the mistaken notion that if we just tell people over and over again what we want, what we believe, or what we don't like, eventually they will change their behavior. We just keep chipping away at the other person, hoping that eventually we will just wear them down and they will do things, see things, or believe things in accordance with our desires.

That's just not what we do in recovery. We get to tell our friends (or our loved ones) how we feel...just once. Living life on life's terms means accepting the fact that not everyone is going to agree with how we feel, or feel compelled to do things our way. The good news is that by acknowledging the right of other people to their own opinions and ways of doing things, we are exposed to ways of thinking that are quite possibly wiser and more effective than our ideas. So if you didn't get what you wanted the first time from your friend, lover, partner, or whatever, maybe it's a sign to stop being his or her majesty, the baby, and allow others the dignity of their points of view.

In the drama of life, we tried to be the director...

JUNE 27
What Do You Get at the Supermarket?

*I*f you said food, beverages, toiletries, and household paper goods, you would only be half right. In addition, you get a lesson in boundaries. When you go into the checkout line, those little rubber boundary thingies separate your stuff from that of the other shoppers. That way, the checkout person knows where the other person's things end and yours begin.

In life, we need clear boundaries between ourselves and other people. We need to know where we end and they begin. We need to know when we have a right to tell people what to do, and when the right thing to do is to back off. In alcoholic homes, though, boundaries become blurred. Alcoholic and addicted parents do not model healthy boundaries for their children, who grow up lacking such boundaries as they seek to navigate adult life.

And if you don't know where your stuff begins and the other person's stuff ends, you're in for a rough road. If I'm going too fast for you, you may want to try Al-Anon. There, you'll learn how to set healthy boundaries with other people, even those who are still practicing their addictions.

Boundaries. They're the only thing at the supermarket that's free.

JUNE 28
Why Resentments Are like Barnacles

I don't know much about boats, but I do know that if they're going to cut through the water, somebody has to scrape all the barnacles that attach to the prow. It sounds like hard, unpleasant work, which means you can include me out. But at the same time, somebody's got to do it if that vessel will cut through the waves with maximum force.

I think of myself as a vessel moving along the river of life. My prow is my attitude, the thing that precedes me into every situation. Barnacles are the resentments that subtly affect my attitude. Thus as a sailor has to scrape those barnacles off the prow of her boat, so I have to keep scraping those resentments away from my attitude.

That's why we have a 10th Step, and not just a 4th Step. The 4th Step is where we look at the grosser handicaps that held us back in the past. The 10th Step is to help us recognize new resentments that occur, so that we can deal with them promptly.

Keep yourself shipshape!

JUNE 29
"I Pushed and God Pulled."

True story. A three-year-old boy, the grandchild of friends of mine, was suffering from a painful bout of constipation. Nothing his parents suggested was working to help the boy, well, do what he needed to do. The parents had tried everything, and then exhausted and exasperated, told him through the closed bathroom door, "Pray."

A few minutes later, the parents heard the sound of a flushing toilet and the little boy emerged from the bathroom happy and relieved.

"I did what you told me! I prayed!" the little boy explained. "I pushed, and God pulled."

Moral of the story: If we want God to pull, we first have to push.

This, too, shall pass.

JUNE 30
An Amend Is Not a Booty Call

Addicts and alcoholics like to probe everything for weaknesses so we can figure out how we can come out ahead on the deal. This tendency to seek out angles even applies to recovery, and nowhere more so than on the 8th and 9th Steps. The purpose of these Steps is to make amends, to set right the wrongs we have done, to restore broken relationships, and thus bring ourselves closer to the spiritual awakening that insures against relapse. But even that isn't enough for us.

We sometimes use the process of making amends as a means of reigniting arguments, as in, "I'm sorry for my behavior, but what you did is even worse." Or as attempts to get rehired. "I'm sorry for what I did, and I really need a job." Or most commonly, the amend-as-booty-call, as in, "I'm sorry for how I cheated on you, and what are you doing tonight?"

This is where our sponsors come in, to help us check our motives. They help ensure that we're only contacting people to whom we caused actual harm. And they keep us from calling back old girl-friends or boyfriends, knowing that we want to turn amends into romantic interludes.

Best not to do anything after you make an amend
that will require an additional amend to that same person.

JULY 1
In Adulthood, There Are No Victims, Only Volunteers

Children can be victims, alas. But once you're an adult, you can only volunteer for victimhood. Do you?

The beginning of maturity is accepting responsibility not just for our actions, but also for the *outcomes or results of those actions.* If I choose to stay in a boring, dead-end job with a nasty boss, at some point I have to stop blaming the boss. If I choose to be in a relationship with an abusive or unloving person, yes, the person may well be abusive or unloving. But nobody is forcing me at gunpoint to stay in that relationship.

It's my responsibility to own what I do and what happens as a result of what I do. Society today, alas, is trending in the other direction. Popular culture teaches victimhood. Otherwise intelligent people encourage others to see themselves as victims and to wallow in their own pain, instead of taking actions to make their lives better.

If you were victimized as a child, I applaud you for doing what you need to do to make your life better. But if you're biologically an adult, and you still think you're a victim? It's time to grow up.

You have no idea how much energy it takes to be a victim...
until you stop being one.

JULY 2
Your Relationship with God Tells You How Happy You Are with Yourself

If you hate the very idea of God, you don't even need to do a 4th Step. I'll share with you the results of what it would be right now: You're full of self-hatred, you're angry, you're frustrated, and you don't believe it's going to get any better. On the other hand, if you have a happy relationship with your Higher Power, you're probably a happy camper, at least most of the time.

As I got healthier in the program, my relationship with my Higher Power got healthier, and as my relationship with my Higher Power improved, I got better. Yet one more reason why it's absurd to think physical sobriety is all you need.

Your Higher Power changes just as you do.

JULY 3
More Will Be Revealed...
or More Will Be Relived

*F*or whatever reason, God chose to make life unfold on a "need to know" basis. Meaning that we don't have all of the facts, even when we have to make an important decision. How will our marriage turn out? The only way we'll find out is by proposing. Will my kid ever straighten up and fly right? Tune in tomorrow.

There's a scene in the classic comedy "When Harry Met Sally" that shows both of them on a split screen, lying in their respective beds, reading the endings of books, because they want to know how things turn out. That may be a natural human desire, but from God's perspective, it's just not how His version of the Game of Life is played.

If we had all the answers, we might not play full on. Life will somehow repeat the extended experience over and over, until we truly get the lesson.

More will be revealed...or more will be relived.

Sought through conscious contact...

JULY 4
Don't Judge Other People's Outsides by Your Insides

You probably have never done this, because you're too serene. But a lot of us will see a stranger who looks more attractive, more fit, better dressed, wealthier, or just more *something* in some important department of life. And based on a quick glimpse, we will concoct a whole life story about this person, as if we were in a Hollywood pitch meeting and not simply living our lives.

In this fantasy we've constructed, these individuals have everything to be happy about. They're rich, successful, beloved, happy, and whatever else we want for ourselves. We make them everything we wish we were. This is part of why I love coming to meetings. I'll see someone like that, judge their outsides by my insides, and create that fabulous life story for them, only to watch the whole thing crumble into dust the first time they open their mouths.

It's only natural when we are drinking or using or new in recovery to judge other people's outsides by our insides. As time goes on, we realize that we have no idea what other people's lives are like, and then we only start to know what their story is once they open up in a meeting.

You're doing great. You just haven't realized it yet.

JULY 5
Don't Dial Pain

Those of us who come from alcoholic families have a fairly low ceiling on how happy we allow ourselves to be. At least that's the case until we get into recovery, and sometimes, even for a while after that. We all know that there are certain people who are just no fun to talk to. They are professional downers, killjoys, wet blankets. Alas, some of them are our relatives.

If it's going to be painful to talk to someone, and you don't really need to talk to that person, why call? Why dial pain? If it's an ex, there's probably a good reason that person is an ex. You don't need to see how they're doing, and you certainly don't owe them, as an A.A. acquaintance of mine once described it, "post-relationship care." Your love does not come with a warranty.

One day in recovery, I realized that I didn't even have enough time for all the functional people in my life, let alone the crazy people I attracted when I was nuts myself. If someone doesn't treat you right, why call? As Quentin Crisp, author of *The Naked Civil Servant*, wrote, "Let the unlovable wash their own dishes." You have a right to be happy, and only you can keep that ceiling on your own happiness. But why would you?

You didn't get clean to stay miserable.

JULY 6
If You Can't Remember Your Last Drink …

…*O*r drug, or substitute…you probably haven't had it yet. The old-timers strongly suggest getting and defending a sobriety date. It's not just about counting days, because that gives a false impression that you can always pick up and just start counting again, and you'll only have lost a week, a month, or whatever.

If, however, you know your sobriety date, you are less likely to drink or use, because you've drawn a line in the sand. You're telling the world that was my last drink or use or activity to date. Generally, the number one reason for *not* setting a sobriety date is that you know you aren't done yet.

When I entered the program, if you asked people how long they had been sober, they would modestly say, "a few twenty-four hours." Today, people will tell you practically to the second, with the help of sobriety date counting apps, precisely how long they have been sober. A sobriety date isn't something to boost one's ego or brag about. It's an internal measure of just how committed one is to staying clean and sober.

Have a sobriety date…and defend it.

JULY 7
Father Dowling Was Right

Father Ed Dowling was one of Bill Wilson's primary influences when he was helping to create Alcoholics Anonymous. You can learn more about him in *A.A. Comes Of Age*, a conference approved book published after the 1950 convention in St. Louis. This is where Bill and Dr. Bob transferred leadership of A.A. from themselves to the A.A. groups around the world, and it's also when the Traditions were first accepted as part of Alcoholics Anonymous. In that book, Father Dowling is quoted as saying that it's the job of people in recovery to *turn over as much as they understand about themselves to as much as they understand about God.*

As we grow in recovery, we come to understand ourselves better, and we have a deeper understanding of our Higher Power as well. It also suggests that no matter what happens in life, seemingly good or seemingly bad, it's our job to turn all of that over to our loving Higher Power, who knows best for us. The process Father Dowling described in those few, powerful words are the task of a lifetime.

Thank you, Father Dowling.

JULY 8
Hundred Dollar Bills ... or Dimes?

When I was new, I got to hear a gentleman in A.A. who had more than thirty years sober at the time. He went by the name of "Dirty Jack" and he had a great way of making things clear as he spoke from the podium.

"If you don't do what A.A. asks you to do," he said, and you're welcome to substitute your own 12-Step program for A.A., "one day, you'll look in your pockets. And where there should have been hundred dollar bills, you'll just find dimes."

He wasn't just talking about money, about the fact that if we don't grow up, get a job, and get serious about life, we are condemning ourselves to financial problems for the rest of our lives. He was also speaking on a metaphorical level. If we don't do the real work involved in spiritual growth, encapsulated in the 12 Steps, we won't even come close to being the people we could have been. Where we could have been "wealthy" from a spiritual standpoint, we will have simply continued to impoverish ourselves.

What's in your wallet?

JULY 9
My Higher Power Invented Sex. What Did Yours Ever Do?

Sometimes people aren't quite sure about this whole Higher Power business. They hear that in 12-Step recovery, you get to define your own concept of God, and the task seems overwhelming. So the suggestion is usually made to borrow the Higher Power of one's sponsor or someone else in the group with longtime sobriety until you have a concept that works for you.

In the spirit of generosity, I would like to make my Higher Power available to anyone reading these words. You don't even have to send an email request. My Higher Power is yours for the taking. If you want to know His credentials, He created the universe, people, animals, planets, galaxies, and sex.

Not to mention the fact that he's been keeping me clean and sober for a very long time, a day at a time.

What has your Higher Power ever done for you?

JULY 10
If the Relationship Didn't Work Then, It Won't Work Now Either

It's gotten really easy to find people to date, hang around with, or just sleep with. The Internet offers a wide variety of apps and methodologies for meeting Mr. or Ms. Right, or Mr. or Ms. Right Now. So why do we addicts and alcoholics spend so much time going back to the ex?

It's familiar. It's comfortable. Maybe it wasn't great, but we aren't really looking for great. We just don't want to be alone. I heard an A.A. speaker from the Pacific Group describe this phenomenon absolutely perfectly. "Getting back into a relationship after it already failed once," he told the audience, "is like taking a second bite out of the same turd."

Serious about having a better life? Then it's time to move on from what didn't work in the past. If it didn't work last time, it's not going to work now, and you may well end up drinking or using over the whole thing. Why expose yourself to relapse, just for the sake of not sleeping alone?

If all your ex's live in Texas, stay out of Texas.

JULY 11
Don't Take Yourself Too, Too Seriously

It's hard to say that phrase, attributed to a longtime Los Angeles A.A. member named George, without smiling. Give it a try. Go ahead. I'll wait.

For people who are willing to throw our lives away with drugs and alcohol, it's amazing how deadly serious (and deadly dull) we can become once we get sober. Everything seems heightened—our highs are incredibly high, and our lows are brutally, miserably low. Maybe one of the best things that can happen to us in recovery is that we find a comfortable middle in life, where we are no longer elated beyond imagining or downright suicidal.

We must take our responsibilities—our recovery, our family responsibilities, our financial and work responsibilities—seriously. But this doesn't mean that we have to think about them to the exclusion of everyone and everything else on the planet.

If you're wrapped up in yourself,
you make a very small package.

JULY 12
You Don't Owe an Amend to Your Dealer

There's only one reason to get in touch with a drug dealer, and that's to buy drugs. Maybe you ripped your drug dealer off mercilessly in the past. It doesn't matter. The only reason for reengaging is that you aren't quite done.

The same thing is true with anyone on our amends list with whom we want to reengage for reasons that are less than pure. Maybe we want to get back together with an ex. Maybe we want to re-litigate an argument we had with someone from our past. So we invent some "harm" that we caused that person, and then we convince ourselves, and sometimes even our sponsors, that we would be perfectly sensible to reach out to this person and start the conversation, the relationship, or the buying and selling again, all in the name of making amends.

I don't buy it, and neither should you. There's only one legitimate reason to make an amend—and that's because you caused that person harm. If you didn't, you're just looking for trouble. And that's something we alcoholics and addicts have majored in from jump street.

Made direct amends to drug dealers whenever possible? Uh, no.

JULY 13
How to Be "A Worker among Workers"

Former Secretary of State Colin Powell wrote in his memoir, *An American Journey*, that when he was a teenager, he worked at the Coca-Cola bottling plant near his home in the Bronx, mopping the floors there after school. It was just a part-time job, but he threw himself into it because that was the nature of the work ethic his parents had instilled in him. The next summer, he went back to see if he could get a job again. He was surprised when the president of the bottling company took him aside and said, "We've never had anybody work as hard at cleaning floors as you."

Alcoholics and addicts, unlike the young Colin Powell, try to find the minimum necessary to skate by in practically any situation, whether it's work, relationships, or even the program. We are by nature half-measures people. But now that we're clean and sober, it's time to scrap that old way of doing things, especially in our work lives where people are paying us for our time.

As soon as you get to work, get to work.

JULY 14
"Group" Stands For "Grow Up"

One of my friends at the Park Street group in Boston used to say that her only excuse for missing her home group was if she was "in a box."

In most major metropolitan areas, you can go to a different meeting every day, sit in the back, and never let anyone get to know you. You might be physically sober, but you're missing out on one of the biggest benefits of 12-Step recovery—the accountability, fellowship, friendship, and pleasure that comes from being a member of a group.

Have at least one home group and maybe a few. Sit up front. Take commitments, so people can get to know you. If your group has activities like putting on meetings in recovery homes or hospitals and institutions, go. Stick around for the business meetings, which may be boring, but are useful because they teach dispute resolution skills to alcoholics and addicts who are typically sorely in need of such skills. And as a speaker down south used to say, "If your group isn't the best group in the whole world, stay there and make it the best group—instead of joining some other group and lousing that one up!"

The individual may drink, but the group stays sober.

JULY 15
"Somebody's Got to Pay for It."

As we say in Al-Anon, just because it has your name on it doesn't mean you have to take it personally. Usually, when people are saying mean things, it has nothing to do with you. You just happen to be in the room, or in the way. The reality is that they are radiating outward their own negative self-image. They don't like themselves, so they're taking it out on you.

Truman Capote wrote a book called *In Cold Blood* about a Kansas family murdered by two angry youths. When the culprits were asked why they did it, they explained that they had had deeply unhappy childhoods and "somebody has to pay for it."

That was hardly a defense that would have won them an acquittal in a court of law back then (although who knows—it might win one today). The short of it is that when someone is being mean to you, it's because they were treated badly and, well, somebody's got to pay for it, so why not you?

So the question should no longer be why are they being so mean to me? The real question is why am I sticking around to take it?

"I didn't come here to be insulted."
"Is that so? Where do you usually go?"

JULY 16
There's No Such Thing as Serenity Plus

The root of so much unhappiness is searching for something that doesn't exist, and doesn't even need to exist. I call it…*serenity plus.*

If I could just wake up in the morning in awe of the fact that I'm alive, that I have the gift of consciousness, that I'm healthy and free, that I live in a time when 12-Step programs are widespread and that I have a way to arrest my disease of alcoholism, and that I actually enjoy long time sobriety in multiple 12-Step programs, shouldn't that be enough?

But, no. Instead, I ignore all that. I ignore the fact that I have four healthy children. I ignore the fact that I went from being on heating assistance to selling my business. All because I'm searching for something more than serenity. I'm searching for serenity plus.

Serenity plus? That's crazy talk.

JULY 17
In the Blue Trunks, Carl Jung, and in the Red Trunks, Sigmund Freud

*H*ow fortunate we are that one of Bill W.'s key spiritual advisors was Carl Jung, who believed that the key to recovery from alcoholism was spiritual. Imagine for a moment if Bill's advisor had instead been Sigmund Freud. In that case, our 4th Step, where we take inventory of our behavior, would have been our 1st Step. A.A. would have been gripped by analysis paralysis from the start.

Things certainly would have been embarrassing when Dr. Bob made his final speech at an A.A. gathering. He told the members to avoid "Freudian complexes" and keep it simple. Freud would not have been amused.

That's why A.A. remains…forever Jung.

JULY 18
You're the Only Copy of <u>The Big Book</u> They May Ever See

As they say in South Boston, when you get sober, your friends and family "have the peeper" on you. They're not saying anything, but they're watching to see if this A.A. or N.A. thing that you've jumped into really works. Maybe they know they need it. Maybe they know *you* need it.

Either way, you may well be the only copy of *The Big Book of Alcoholics Anonymous* that your family, friends, coworkers, neighbors, and fellow drivers ever see. So in a sense, once you're sober and people know it, you become an ambassador for the fellowship. People are going to judge the efficacy and legitimacy of the program based on your actions. It may not be fair, but life isn't fair.

As Earl Nightingale said, "What you do speaks so loudly I can hardly hear a word you're saying." This is especially true for friends and family who are witnessing your rebirth as you commit to the 12 Steps and living a clean and sober life. Are you staying off the booze and drugs? Are you a better person? Or is it all a bunch of hot air?

Represent.

JULY 19
Of the Educational Variety

Whenever I read Bill's story, I find myself envious of his white light experience at Towns Hospital. In a seemingly hopeless state of alcoholic collapse, Bill cried out, "If there is a God, let him reveal Himself to me now!" Sure enough, the room filled with white light and Bill found himself transfixed...and ultimately transformed. He never drank again.

Why couldn't I have had a white light experience just like Bill, I ask sadly. And then I remember...I did. I was seventeen-years-old, at Jones Beach in New York, suffering from "Senioritis"—a disease known only to second semester high school seniors, who find themselves at the beach instead of in class on warm spring days.

I had a book with me by the philosopher Abraham Joshua Heschel. He was writing about the glories of nature and how they revealed the hand of God. I looked at the words on the page, and then out at the sparkling, sun-kissed ocean. Then back at the waves. And back at the ocean. And I felt it. A white light experience of my very own. Of course, I drank for another fifteen years, so in some sense, the whole white light thing was wasted on me. But at least I can say I had one.

Have you seen the light yet?

JULY 20
The Trouble with Perfection

The alcoholics and addicts are often perfectionists, although usually we're too lazy to put the work in to achieve perfection. So the natural question is why we consider perfection such an important goal. I once heard a woman in a meeting say, "I wanted to understand my perfectionism, so I looked up the word in the dictionary, and it said, 'Beyond criticism.'

That's when I realized all I ever wanted was for people to stop criticizing me."

I thought about that for a long time and I realized that the strategy felt flawed. Even if you are perfect or do something perfectly, whether it's cooking a perfect meal, doing a perfect job at work, or whatever, the people who you're trying to get to stop criticizing you are too imperfect themselves to notice how perfect you are.

In short, perfectionism is a failed strategy for avoiding criticism.

In 12-Step recovery, the only thing you have to do perfectly is the 1st Step—not drink or use. And even if you do pick up, just come back.

The great news is that we don't have to be perfect to be perfectly wonderful.

Don't go changing to try and please me.

JULY 21
The World Will Stop Calling You an Alcoholic or Addict . . .

... *t*he minute you stop calling yourself one.

Alcoholics and addicts of all ages mistakenly believe that no one else knows what they're doing. There's even a term for it—a bubble. We think we're hiding the booze, the drugs, the pills, the food, the prostitutes, or whatever. In reality, everybody knows everything. The secret's out.

The good news is that we live in a forgiving society—witness the often choreographed but almost always accepted apologies of celebrities who mess up. Fortunately, what works for them works for us. Once we are able to take the 1st Step and acknowledge our addiction, no matter what kind, the world forgives, forgets, and moves on.

Your teenage kids may need a little more time to adjust to the new you, but if you give them that time, even they will eventually forgive you.

Funny how we're the last to know
that everyone else already knew.

JULY 22
The Serenity Prayer Is a Prayer, Not Just a Thing to Say While Holding Hands with Strangers

The Serenity Prayer is something that is said, usually without much consideration for the meaning of the words, at the beginning or end of many 12-Step meetings.

The origin of the prayer is an interesting piece of A.A. lore. Somebody saw it in an obituary in a newspaper around 1944 or so and sent it in to the A.A. office in New York, where Nell Wing, Bill's secretary, put it on his desk. Bill was so taken with the prayer, which was composed by the great theologian, Reinhold Niebuhr, that he popularized it in Alcoholics Anonymous.

We recite it by rote so frequently that we often forget that it's actually a request that we are making of our Higher Power. We are asking for serenity, but we are so distracted that we even forgot we wanted it. And how do we get serenity? By remembering the difference between the things we can change (our words and our actions) and the things we cannot change (everyone and everything else).

Don't just say the Serenity Prayer—
Pray the Serenity Prayer.

JULY 23
What God Can Handle

*O*nce, I heard an A.A. speaker sober for twenty years whose words and demeanor reflected the humility the program can instill in us. "I don't feel like I'm really the right person to change the literature," he began, "because it says 'God doesn't give us more than we can handle.'

"But I was told that we're supposed to give everything to God, the good and the bad. So for me, it's 'God doesn't give us anything that *God* can't handle.'"

I admired his humility, and I admired his thinking even more. What a beautiful idea—that no matter what comes along, it's our responsibility to give it to God, because whatever it is, God can certainly handle it.

If I could put that speaker's change to a vote, I'm sure it would win in a landslide.

If God can't handle it, nobody can.

JULY 24
A Bridge to Nowhere

*P*hysician and author Deepak Chopra tells a story in one of his books about an American couple visiting India. Near their hotel, they see a handsome, physically fit young man sitting under a bridge—and they continue to see him in that same place every day of their trip. Finally, on the last day, they approach the young man and ask him what he is doing.

"Here in India," he explained calmly, "We believe in reincarnation. So I am sitting this life out."

Here in the West, some of us believe in reincarnation and some of us don't. But regardless of how you feel about it, why take the chance that you won't get another chance at life?

This life may be the only one that we get here on Earth, regardless of what we believe may precede or follow our human incarnation.

What are you doing with your precious time on this lovely planet? Are you actively involved in your own recovery, creating, building, learning, and giving? Or are you sitting this life out?

Sitting under a bridge takes its toll.

JULY 25
Buying Carpenters' Tools
Doesn't Make You a Carpenter

A.A. speaks of the "inner spiritual tools" that we lay at the feet of the newcomer. By laying them at their feet, newcomers have to bend over to pick them up. While down there, they might hit their knees, and ask for help. It could happen.

But just because you have tools doesn't mean you are instantly adept at using them, or that you're going to get results from them right away. The A.A. toolbox is filled with great ideas about how to live one's life, stay sober, and get happy, but like all tools, they take practice.

The good news is that when we are using spiritual tools, we are no longer trying to fix a glass table with a hammer, which is how most of us used to go through life.

Put down the toys and pick up the tools.

JULY 26
To Get the Big Picture, Take a Few Steps Back

My sponsor, Milton, liked to compare our lives to a tapestry, a beautiful blend of rich hues with a wonderful design. The problem is that if you stand too close to a tapestry, all you see are seemingly random threads that don't appear to be connecting with anything else or leading anywhere. We have to take a few steps back to see the tapestry in all its glory.

The same thing is true with our lives. In any given moment, we don't have enough perspective to judge whether a particular event is good or bad. We jump to conclusions, usually making ourselves unhappy in the process. Take a few steps back, however, get some perspective, and suddenly the richness of our experience becomes clear.

Get the big picture.

JULY 27
Everybody Surrenders to Something

Twelve-Step programs make a point of asking members to surrender, but in reality, we are always surrendering to something. If we're drinking and driving, we're surrendering to the police. If we're convicted of a crime, we're surrendering to the prison system. If we're drinking or using, we are surrendering to our addiction.

We always have a choice to surrender to our lower Higher Power, our addictions, or our higher Higher Power, which is God as you understand God. We don't have a choice about surrendering—we're always surrendering to something. So as long as we *are* surrendering, we might as well make the best choice.

Surrender means joining the winning side.

JULY 28
You, on the Rocks

*D*an Sullivan, founder of the Strategic Coach program for entre-preneurs, writes that cliff divers in Mexico must time their dives to begin when they see the rocks below, not the water. If a diver starts her dive when water is visible, the result will be a fatal accident. Of course, it takes a lot more courage to dive when you only see rocks.

In our own lives, it's when we think we're going to end up "on the rocks" that we must make our move. Faith means taking action when you have no guarantee of success. The good news is that the program works. It works for other people, and it will work for you as well.

Take the leap.

☕

JULY 29
Powerless Doesn't Mean Impotent

A lot of people don't like the word *powerless*, because it makes them feel, well, powerless. Admitting that we are powerless over alcohol, drugs, or some other substance or behavior is hard. But there's humility and, yes, even power, in the decision to admit one's powerlessness. Shame isn't the inability to handle booze or alcohol. The shame is trying to prove to yourself or others that you can keep on using, when common sense, the evidence of a lifetime, and maybe even the police and the courts are telling you otherwise.

Only when you admit powerlessness over a substance or behavior can you actually tap into the power that you find in the Program—the power of the group, the power of relationships with a sponsor, the power of God. The declaration of powerlessness is the way to tap into power sources, both seen and unseen, and that's how recovery begins.

Powerless doesn't mean impotent.
It also doesn't mean clueless.

JULY 30
Don't "Should" on Yourself

Addicts, alcoholics, and Al-Anons love to "should" on ourselves. We *should* drop fifteen pounds. We *should* go to more meetings. We *should* find a new boyfriend. We *should* get a better job. And on and on, until we're just sick of ourselves.

At some point—and why not right now?—we are entitled to cease loading ourselves up with all these "shoulds." If you think you're supposed to do something, just go do it. Don't sit there and agonize about it. If you "should" go to a meeting, then go to the meeting. If you should drop fifteen pounds, stop eating white flour and white sugar right now. This minute. Do what you need to do, instead of making yourself crazy.

Life will go on whether you lose the fifteen pounds or not, whether you go to the meeting or not, whether you get a better job or not, or whether you find that new boyfriend or not. It will certainly be a lot better if you take the steps to make those things a reality, if they are on your to-do list. But for God's sake, stop shoulding on yourself. Do it or don't do it, but don't sit there in agony over whether you "should" or not.

Should or get off the pot.

JULY 31
"No Way to Correct Nothing."

In his magisterial study of the building of the Panama Canal, *The Path Between the Seas: The Creation of the Panama Canal*, David McCullough quoted the superintendent on the project, John Stevens, as saying the following: "Do something. If it is wrong, you can correct that, but there is no way to correct nothing."

According to McCullough, until Teddy Roosevelt and John Stevens came on the scene, the Panama Canal had been mired in mishaps, disease, and failure lasting decades. Stevens' attitude—do something, because you can always go back to fix it later—made the difference.

That's not the worst idea when it comes to sobriety. If you take an action, there's every possibility that you'll either succeed or that you can course correct. If you don't do anything, well, you can't expect much.

Wayne Gretzky is quoted as saying "You miss 100% of the shots you don't take." And legendary UCLA basketball coach, John Wooden, would say, "The team that makes the most mistakes usually wins."

Do something.

AUGUST 1
I'm Crazy, But How Can I Tell?

The Big Book of Alcoholics Anonymous speaks of the "subtle insanity" that precedes the first drink. What a brilliant turn of phrase! Typically, insanity is florid, obvious, undeniable. But when it's subtle, I don't even notice how crazy I am.

When alcoholics and addicts begin to feel uncomfortable, the desire is to quiet those feelings as quickly as possible. When we are in our disease, we do so with alcohol, drugs, spending, inappropriate sexual relations, food, debting, and the like. In recovery, it is possible to dissipate that subtle insanity through healthy actions. Calling your sponsor. Calling a newcomer. Praying. Reading literature. Writing about resentments and fears, or as Milton used to say, just having a sandwich and a nap.

There's nothing in 12-Step recovery to remedy the gross insanity that follows the first drink. But as long as we keep taking the right actions, we can gently nudge that subtle insanity out of our immediate thinking, so it's not necessary to pick up or act out.

"If we couldn't laugh, we'd all go insane."
—Jimmy Buffett

AUGUST 2
If You Start Your Day on Your Knees...

... *t*hen life can't drive you to your knees.

Life is hard. It's complicated, and it requires alcoholics and addicts to do the one thing they find harder than anything else—to get along with others. Sometimes we think that by getting sober, we have a shield against any sort of bad thing ever happening to us again as long as we live. That's not true. We can still have health issues, money issues, relationship issues, or all the other challenges of life, normal and abnormal. The only difference is that, by the grace of our Higher Power, we don't have to drink or use over those things.

That's why it's so important for me to take my sponsor's suggestion and start my day by hitting my knees. It's an act of humility that reminds me that I'm not running the show. It also allows me to "rejoin" Alcoholics Anonymous by reminding myself, and my Higher Power, that I am an alcoholic and I need to be kept from the first drink for the first day.

Turn it over.

AUGUST 3
The Disease Is Progressive, but So Is Recovery

You don't really need to be an expert in the disease of alcoholism to understand one core fact—the disease gets worse over time, never better. It's easy to see why—the longer you keep drinking or drugging, the more of that substance your body needs in order to experience the effect you desire. And at the same time, the more you drink or use, the more you break down the body's ability to process drugs and alcohol. Despair increases, we get shunned by all but the hard-core addicts in our world, and nothing good happens.

Conversely, recovery is also progressive. The longer you stay clean and sober, the more good things come along. You become employable again. You become someone that people want to have around, date, or marry. Tax, legal, and criminal issues get resolved. It's a gaining game.

Addiction and recovery are both like the shark—
they're always moving forward. Are you?

AUGUST 4
If You're Happy Within, You Can Be Happy Without

Alcoholics and addicts are famous for trying to fill God-sized holes with money, property, prestige, food, sex, comfort, and every other material thing or physical experience you can think of.

One of the men in my home group had just one lung. He didn't have a lot of money, either. But he sure seemed a lot happier than the rest of us, all of whom had two lungs.

We live in a materialist, consumerist society. There's nothing wrong with having nice stuff—it's great. But a lot of wealthy people can tell you, from bitter experience, that just simply having stuff never filled that God-sized hole.

You can rent pleasure, but you can't buy happiness.

AUGUST 5
Happiness Is a Good Attitude and a Bad Memory

Wouldn't you hate to be judged for something you said or did yesterday, last week, or last year? That's how the people in your world—your spouse or partner, your kids, your parents, your coworkers, everybody—feel about you. With sobriety, we come to realize that we were always doing the best we could. It's just that a lot of the time, we did a lousy job. In sobriety, we get to do a better job. We still aren't going to be perfect, because life isn't a game of perfect. We are going to make mistakes, slip up, and say or do the wrong thing.

But just as we might wish others to forgive and forget, we have to extend that same courtesy to our fellows. Make it a point of waking up every morning and giving everyone in your world a clean slate. Don't drag yesterday's resentments into today's encounters. If you can be as patient with the people around you as your Higher Power is with you, you're on your way to having a very good day.

If you don't judge, you never have to forgive.

AUGUST 6
"Just Change Everything!
Hahaha!"

One of my least favorite "jokes" that gets repeated by recovering alcoholics and addicts is, "All you have to do is come here and change everything, ha, ha, ha!"

That's not funny.

If I could have changed anything, I would never have come in to 12-Step recovery. Fact is, I couldn't change *anything*—my behavior, my attitude, my drinking, my anger, my inability to hold a job, my poor relationships with family members—none of it.

The good news is that if I am willing to take the Steps, I will be changed by them.

I had to change a few things—from not going to meetings to going to meetings; from not having or using a sponsor to having a sponsor; from having nothing to do with the Steps to taking and then living the Steps.

And by making those changes, everything else fell into place.

Now that's change you can believe in.

AUGUST 7
Make Your Short-Term Goal Noon and Your Long-Term Goal Midnight

Goals are important. Alcoholics and addicts are often high achievers, at least when we're not drinking and using, so we like to set goals. When we're new, however, since this is a one day at a time program, our short-term goal ought to be noon and our long-term goal, midnight. This way, we are aiming for the pillow sober and we aren't getting confused or distracted. And then the next day, we wake up and do the same thing all over again—short-term goal, noon; long-term goal, midnight.

I once heard a successful business executive say at an A.A. meeting, "I've always had yearly, quarterly, and monthly goals. But now that I'm sober, my goals are Steps 10, 11, and 12."

It's still how I try to live my life today. If it happens outside a meeting, it ought to be none of my business.

Aim high.

AUGUST 8
Whatever ... Enough

The sponsor told the newcomer, "Every morning, when you open your eyes, look up at the ceiling and say, 'Whatever.' And then just before you go to sleep, say, 'Enough.'" So the sponsee did that. Day after day. Whatever. Enough. Whatever. Enough.

After a couple of weeks, the sponsee couldn't take it anymore.

"Enough," he cried to his sponsor. "Whatever," the sponsor replied.

If you can look up to your Higher Power and say, "whatever"—if you're truly open to whatever comes along instead of trying to control outcomes or force life to live up to your expectations—you've reached a level of serenity that is far beyond anything I've experienced.

The ability to say to one's Higher Power, "whatever," is huge. And then by saying, "enough," it means that you're able to turn off the thinking machine that is your mind and get a good night's sleep. And then you start again the next day.

Whatever works.

AUGUST 9
How to Never Get Cut Off on the Highway

Years ago, I was at a meeting when a man put up his hand and said, "I haven't been cut off on the highway since I got sober thirty-two years ago. Here's my secret: I let them in."

It's amazing how aggressive we alcoholics and addicts can be behind the wheel. Where are we going that requires us to drive with such speed and fury? It's not like we like our jobs, if we still have a job, or that we're all that crazy about our family members. So where exactly are we racing? To the dealer man? Understandable. Anywhere else? I give up.

When I got sober, I realized I no longer needed to be the fastest car on the highway. I came to recognize that a car with a turning signal on was not asking permission to come into "my" lane. Instead, the turning signal was a piece of information—they were coming into a lane that belonged to all of us.

Just because you drive people crazy doesn't mean you also have to drive crazy.

AUGUST 10
Every Bottom Has a Trap Door

It doesn't matter how far down the scale we have gone—we can always go lower. So in A.A., we don't say, "I haven't done that." Instead, we say, "I haven't done that...yet."

We talk about the *yets* as the behaviors, choices, criminal charges, or other problems that alcoholics can get into, but they just simply haven't touched our lives... yet. The good news is that you don't have to take the elevator all the way to the sub-basement. If you've been digging your own grave with alcohol, drugs, and the like, the smartest move would be to put down the shovel.

How low can you go?

AUGUST 11
Out of the Boxcar

*D*an Sullivan, the founder of the Strategic Coach program, tells the story of a boxcar in Nazi Germany that had just been filled with prisoners headed for a concentration camp. One of the unfortunates onboard noticed that the wood at the base of the train car wall nearest him was rotting and vulnerable. He started kicking vigorously at it, realizing that as long as the train was still in the city, the noises of the city would mask the sounds of his kicking.

The other passengers, horrified, told him to stop because they could be killed for what he was doing. He reasoned with them that they were going to be killed anyway and this was his only chance. He broke through, and when the train reached the countryside, he chose the right moment, dove through the opening he had created, and survived.

If you are still drinking or using, you might as well be on that same train, because it's not going to end well. This is the time to kick with all of your might, break through what's rotten, and flee to safety.

On the wrong track?

AUGUST 12
If Life Were Fair, You'd Be Broke and Probably Dead

*E*ver notice that when a child thinks the other kid is getting something more, he always says, "That's not fair!" Never "That's wrong"—just "That's not fair!" In other words, we all seem to be born with an idea that life is supposed to be fair. Wrong. If life were fair, then we would be like pretty much everyone else on the planet, eking out a subsistence existence and living on less than two or three dollars a day.

Life isn't fair. Some people have more money, better health, more successful careers, or happier family lives than others. The question is not, why isn't life fair? The better questions are, what do I have to do to attain the things in life I desire? And can I be happy along the way? It's amazing how when it comes to joy, we can all be procrastinators.

And when we do compare ourselves with others, we tend only to compare ourselves with people who have more than we do. There are a lot of people who wish they had what we had, but we never think about them.

Life may not be fair, but it can still be great.

AUGUST 13
If Venting Solved Problems, Complainers Would Be Happy Campers

"I gave him a piece of my mind." Haven't we all said that at one time or another?

At this point in my life, though, I wish I could get all those pieces of my mind back.

We have this crazy idea that if we vent about our troubles, we end up feeling better, as if it were a room full of musty air that just needs an open window. In reality, venting accomplishes nothing. It may influence other people around us to complain as well, and it won't be long until the entire conversation has become totally useless to all parties. Will Bowen wrote a book called *A Complaint Free World*. He says venting doesn't make people happier—and the people who complain frequently are generally the most miserable.

Carry the message to your meeting,
but carry the mess to your sponsor.

AUGUST 14
What Are You Running From?

*O*ne time, I was at the gym, and a trainer whom I knew from A.A. meetings walked by. "What are you running from?" he asked me. I had to laugh. What *was* I running from? My past? An unhappy childhood? Broken relationships? Business failures? Or all of the above?

Most of us spend so much time running from the things we don't want to be or memories we don't want to face that we stop thinking about what we want to run toward. Doesn't it make more sense to run toward something you want instead of trying to run away from thoughts and feelings? Maybe we're just giving those thoughts, feelings, and memories way too much power. That's something we can address with our sponsors.

In Hebrew, the word for "will" is the same as the word for running—in other words, your will is what you run toward. It's probably a good idea for you and your Higher Power to be running in the same direction.

Better question: What are you running to?

AUGUST 15
A Blue Ocean Strategy

*M*any resentments ago, I was the secretary of my home Al-Anon group in Beverly Hills, California, and something happened in the group one day that got me fighting mad. So I called Central Office and demanded proof that I was right and the other member was dead wrong.

The person at Central Office was nice as pie. When she asked for my home address, so she could mail me the relevant pamphlet, I told her I lived in Marina Del Rey, California. "Oh, it's so pretty there," she exclaimed, "especially on mornings when you can see the phosphorescence on the water. You're so lucky to live there." *Yeah, whatever,* I thought. *Just send me the pamphlet.*

A manila envelope from Central Service arrived a few days later, and I tore into it, super excited to receive the evidence that would allow me to put the other Al-Anon member in his place. And attached to the pamphlet was a handwritten note: "Remember to watch for the phosphorescence." Suddenly I forgot all about my upset with the other member. I realized I'd wasted three days chewing on this resentment when instead I could have been looking out the window of my living room, watching for the phosphorescence.

When you can gaze at the ocean,
you don't have to make waves.

AUGUST 16
The Presence of Tragedy
Does Not Disprove the Existence of God

When I reached the 8th and 9th Steps, I realized that I could not blame God for the things that I had done to other people. I did them. Similarly, I realized that I could not blame God for the things that had happened to me or to my loved ones. These were acts by individuals who were misusing their free will.

Tragedy can be a teacher. A famous British author traveled to Africa and saw a boy suffering from a particularly heinous illness and concluded that if there were a God, this would never have happened. But who are we to know? Maybe God owes us an explanation for why He permits tragedy, but just because tragedy exists doesn't mean that God doesn't exist.

The believer only has to explain the existence of God.
The atheist has to explain everything else.

AUGUST 17
If You Had a Watch, You Weren't Ready

When I was newly sober, I came to an Alcoholics Anonymous meeting wearing a watch. The old-timers at the table laughed at me. "Back in the day, they would never have let you in if you were wearing a watch," they said.

"Why?" I asked.

"Because you still had something to lose."

By the time the *12 and 12—Alcoholics Anonymous' 12 Steps and 12 Traditions*—was published in 1952, A.A. no longer specialized solely in high-bottom drunks. The good news is that you don't have to ride the elevator all the way to the bottom to make the decision to get clean and sober.

"If you're a boozer, you're a loser"—that's what one of the old-timers used to say at my home group. The more you booze, the more you lose. Every bottom has a trap door, and if you keep drinking or using, eventually you'll be nostalgic for the misery that you felt today.

Lost enough yet?

AUGUST 18
Two Kinds of Crazy

Alcoholics Anonymous speaks of the "subtle insanity" that precedes the first drink. That subtle insanity lies in sharp contrast with the gross insanity that follows the first drink.

I love the phrase "subtle insanity" because typically we think of insane actions or behaviors as larger than life, out there, and clearly visible. But with alcoholism, a "subtle foe" in the words of *The Big Book*, the insanity that precedes the first drink is indeed subtle.

It's the job of the recovering alcoholic or addict to remain in fit spiritual condition and thus push that subtle insanity off into the future, a day at a time. If we don't, the insanity that follows the first drink is anything but subtle, as it can involve everything from loss of relationships, jobs, family, health, freedom, or our lives.

You can call your sponsor before or after you pick up.
Probably better to call before.

AUGUST 19
Why You Can't "Fire" Your Sponsor

You can always change sponsors. You can make the change because your sponsor is unavailable, not living the values you hoped he or she demonstrated, or for a million other reasons. But you can't fire your sponsor, because your sponsor doesn't work for you! He or she isn't getting paid!

Sponsorship is for fun and for free. Your sponsor is willing to take your call, and will probably come over in the middle of the night if you're afraid that you're about to pick up. Your sponsor serves you with no expectation of reward. The real reward of sponsorship is enhancing one's own program and seeing the light come on in the eyes of others.

You can change sponsors, but you can't fire your sponsor, because you never hired them.

Call your sponsor today.
They love to hear from strangers!

AUGUST 20
Can You Give Up
All Hope of a Happier Yesterday?

*I*n his book, *The Road Less Stupid*, author and businessman Keith Cunningham writes that an employee approached Atari's CEO, Nolan Bushnell, with a proposition. "I'll sell you one-third of the new company I'm starting for $40,000," the employee said.

"Steve," Bushnell replied, "get back to work."

The employee: Steve Jobs. The company: Apple. That fifty-thousand dollars today would be worth billions. Don't you think Nolan Bushnell regrets that decision?

We all have regrets—the house we sold too soon, the job we didn't take, the person we should have married but didn't (or the person we shouldn't have but did). Life is not a game of perfect, and yet many of us spend so much time steeped in frustration over decisions we took that turned out not to be optimal.

Becoming happy today requires us to give up all thought of a happier yesterday. As an A.A. mentor of mine, John R., put it, "The gold ring comes around more than once."

When you stop regretting, you start living.

AUGUST 21
I Don't Know What You Said, but I Know What I Heard

Alcoholics and addicts are often lousy listeners. In one of his mystery novels, author Lawrence Block observed that the way alcoholics "listen" is to wait for the other person to stop speaking, so they can start. Lousy listening leads to misunderstandings and upsets.

"I told you I would be late." "I didn't hear you say that." And they're off, with yet another pointless argument.

The best way to listen is with your eyes. Focus directly on the other person—I don't mean stare them down, but get a good look at them as they speak. It's amazing how much you can hear when you actually pay attention.

Can you hear me now?

AUGUST 22
My First 10th Step

My first Al-Anon sponsor, Harv told me to buy a three-section spiral notebook when we reached Step 10. He told me that there were three categories of things he wanted me to write down every night before I went to bed.

The first was a "did well" list. He told me to write down a list of everything I did well that day, whether it was simply driving to the store, returning a library book, or emptying the dishwasher. People new to recovery need to remind ourselves, he said, that we are actually capable of doing things right. Then, in the second section, he had me create a gratitude list. He told me to put down ten items the first day and add at least three every day going forward, because whatever we pay attention to grows.

The third section was to be a list of people, places, and things over which I have no control. He told me to add one every day. Sometimes it would be the same person for three or four days in a row. He was trying to teach me the concept of boundaries—where I began and where the other person ended. I did that type of 10th Step for years. It definitely changed the way I viewed myself and my life. Feel free to give it a shot.

Life is lived forward but is understood backwards.

AUGUST 23
Yesterday Ended Last Night

Motivational speaker and author extraordinaire Zig Ziglar popularized that phrase. Not everything goes our way, and maybe you had a bad day yesterday. It happens. It makes sense to acknowledge the reality of the "emotional hangover"—the fatigue or even exhaustion we can feel when we had an emotionally charged day. But we must remember that yesterday ended last night—that whatever happened yesterday presumably isn't fatal, because here we are today. We're still in the game.

In basketball, when a team misses a shot and gets the rebound, the shot clock resets and the announcer calls out, "They got a new twenty-four!" This morning, you also received a new twenty-four. What are you doing with it?

Get your head in the game.

AUGUST 24
A Simpler 10th Step

At the International A.A. Convention in San Diego in 1995, I heard a speaker with forty-nine years describe how he did the 10th Step.

"As I lay in bed at night, I imagine that a blackboard descends from above. I take a piece of chalk and write down on one side of the blackboard all the good things that happened over the course of the day. On the other side, I write down all the bad things that happened that day. Then I take an imaginary wet eraser, erase the whole board, send it up heavenward, and go to sleep."

Anything they did in Alcoholics Anonymous in the 1940s is probably a pretty good idea. Try the imaginary blackboard approach for a few nights and see if you sleep better. Of course, not having that extra cup of coffee with dinner and surfing news sites for an hour just before bed will also probably help.

Did I mention the speaker had forty-nine years?

AUGUST 25
"Why Would _You_ Envy Me?"

_M_enachem Mendel Schneerson, known to the world as the Lubavitcher Rebbe, once met a nineteen-year-old who had just gotten into recovery from drug addiction.

The Rebbe's response: "I envy you."

"Why would you envy me?" the young man asked, surprised.

"I'll never go on a journey like yours," the Rebbe said. "I'll never get to experience the growth that you're about to experience. So I envy you."

Just joining us? I envy you.

AUGUST 26
FOMO

FOMO stands for Fear Of Missing Out, also known as the Facebook Effect. People check their social media and see that their friends are eating nice desserts in restaurants, taking great trips, or otherwise looking like they're having more fun. Since when is it necessary to turn our entire lives into clickbait? As Descartes would have said, "I get likes; therefore I am."

The downside of constantly seeing all the pleasure that everyone else seems to be enjoying is to think that our own lives are dull and unhappy by comparison. Social media, and especially Facebook, are time sumps—there are so many better ways to use our precious minutes on Earth than to continually score the dopamine hits we receive when we bombard ourselves with new data on Facebook.

Why make yourself miserable by giving yourself the sense that you're missing out on life? In reality, the time you spend on social media is time during which you really are missing out. As the author of *The Naked Civil Servant*, Quentin Crisp, said, "Don't try to keep up with the Joneses. Instead, drag them down to your level."

If you're clean and sober, you aren't missing anything.

AUGUST 27
Are You in the Flow?

I once heard an A.A. speaker say, "The hand that's most open to give is the hand that's most open to receive." Sobriety and recovery are all about creating a healthy sense of flow in our lives. We give love; we receive love. We serve others; others serve us.

The opposite approach to life is to hoard, to selfishly deprive those around us of the love, support, kind words, and smiles they need in order to thrive or just simply get through the day. The problem is that we cannot deprive others without hurting ourselves. It's awfully tough for your Higher Power to give you anything if your hand is clenched so tightly that you cannot receive.

Sometimes people describe 12-Step fellowships by saying, "It's a selfish program." No. Drinking and using is a selfish program. Recovery is a self-caring situation in which we learn to receive and give. *The Big Book* invites us to see what we can pack into the flow of life.

No, it isn't better to give than to receive.
It's best to do both.

AUGUST 28
Do I Have To? No, You Don't

A.A. meetings have sadly turned into an agglomeration of weird customs that make no sense to the newcomer (or to me). For example, most people "chime in" at the end of readings—examples include "over our own lives" in Al-Anon or "God could and would if he were sought" in A.A.

According to Clancy I., founder of the Midnight Mission in Los Angeles, that whole "chiming in" thing started when a group in the San Fernando Valley started making fun of a frequently inebriated member who would recite the readings along with the speaker. They were doing that to make fun of him, and yet somehow the concept has caught on worldwide in A.A.

Similarly, you don't have to say "Hear, hear" after the speaker says the thing about "Whom you see here…"—nor do you have to take a newcomer chip if you are new.

All you have to do in a 12-Step meeting is…nothing, really. Listening is a good idea, but even if you sleep through the meeting, that's an hour when you weren't drinking or using.

If it seems stupid, don't do it.

AUGUST 29
The Steps Are Not Enough

Some people in 12-Step programs have the mistaken notion that the Steps are all you need in life and that going for outside help is stupid. They are completely wrong.

The Steps were never meant to be a one-size-fits-all solution to life's problems. There's not a lot in the Steps about handling money, or love relationships, or coming to terms with physical or sexual abuse, or a thousand other critical topics.

The Big Book even specifies that we should seek outside help from qualified professionals when appropriate. Your sponsor or that loudmouth in the room might think he is a therapist, a marriage counselor, a credit repair service, or a Harvard-trained psycho-pharmacologist. He's probably just a blowhard who finds pleasure in telling other people what to do.

Twelve-Step programs have the humility to acknowledge that they do not have all the answers. Yet sometimes some of our members, lacking humility, believe they know what's best for you, for them-selves, and everybody in the room. Don't fall for it.

Get outside help.

AUGUST 30
Why Am I Talking?

You cannot get in trouble for what you're thinking, but you can certainly get in trouble for what you say. In the Talmud, in the tractate called Ethics of the Fathers, which was originally written as advice to judges, it says, "All my life, I have grown up among the great thinkers, and I have learned that there is nothing better than silence."

Good advice 2,300 years ago when it was written; even better advice now in the age of social media. Twelve-Step programs have great acronyms. One that comes into play here is W.A.I.T., which stands for, "Why Am I Talking?"

There's a longer version of this, that basically says, "Does what I want to say need to be said? Does it need to be said by me? Does it need to be said right now?" I find that hard to remember. I find W.A.I.T. much easier because it reminds me of what I should do instead of talking. I should just wait until the urge to talk passes.

Silence is fabulous. It lets you see what the other person has to say, and it keeps you out of trouble.

W.A.I.S.T.: Why Am I Still Talking?

AUGUST 31
Two Approaches to Step 2

There are (at least) two approaches to Step 2. Some people come to the first mention of a Higher Power in Alcoholics Anonymous or a different 12-Step program and are fine with it. They've always had a good relationship with a Higher Power, and they're often pleased to see that that relationship will pay dividends here in 12-Step land. And then there's the rest of us.

When I got to my first 12-Step program, I viewed God as a motorcycle cop hiding behind a billboard, waiting to catch you speeding or doing something else wrong. I'm not one of those people who came easily to the idea that a Higher Power could help me with my sobriety. For people like me, there's a great expression—came, came to, came to believe.

Came—Started showing up at meetings.

Came to—Realized I had been living life unconsciously.

Came to believe—Slowly, over time, and not in an instant.

Fortunately, my Higher Power was patient with me and didn't seem to mind that it took a while for me to get to the party.

If you will not pray,
then you don't have a prayer.

SEPTEMBER 1
Sponsorship Expires along with the Sponsee

One day, one of my A.A. buddies called and said that a sponsee of his had passed away, but he was still getting lots of calls from his family members, who were not members of Alcoholics Anonymous. "I'm honored that they call," he said, "but I don't know what I have to offer them. And it's taking up a lot of time."

I suggested to him the idea that in 12-Step recovery, sponsorship expires along with the sponsee.

In other words, if the sponsee passes away, we're very sad, but we do not become a free therapist for the bereaved family. We serve as sponsors "for fun and for free"—because we know the only way we can keep the program is to share it. But with whom do we share it? With other members of our program.

We cannot be all things to all people. We cannot, and should not, even be all things to our sponsees. We are not a job finding service, a therapist, a dating website, a bank, or a source of advice. And when it comes to the family members? We have to butt out. It's just not our role.

We don't play God to our fellows,
in or out of the program.

SEPTEMBER 2
"I'm Such a People Pleaser."

Contrary to popular opinion, people-pleasing is not a character defect. As my late, great sponsor, Milton, used to say, "We were put on Earth to please each other. The problem comes when we are trying to please the other person in order to manipulate them in some way."

Alcoholics, addicts, and Al-Anons are legendary for approaching life as if it were a game of three-dimensional chess. *If I do this for you, you'll do this for me, and then that person will do this for him, and he'll do that for her, and she'll do that for me*...and so on, until it's just exhausting.

If you can do something nice for the other person without any strings attached, you're living life the right way. People-pleasing is not a character defect. It's why we're here. Manipulation, on the other hand, is a character defect, or as Milton would have said, a "bad habit."

So just stop doing it.

What can I do for you?

SEPTEMBER 3
When Should I Open My Parachute?

When the people look like ants, it's too soon. When the ants look like people, it's too late.

Speaking of parachutes…my sponsor Milton used to tell a story about a retired fighter pilot. He was sitting in a restaurant having dinner with his wife when a man his age approached the table. "You flew fighter jets off the deck of the USS Ridgeway," the man said. "You had more than two hundred missions, and you returned safely to the deck of the carrier every single time. You're one of the most decorated Navy fliers in the history of the nation."

The ex-fighter jock was dumbfounded. "How do you know so much about me?" He asked, amazed.

"I packed your parachute," the man said humbly.

Becoming successful is seldom a solo affair. There are most likely a lot of people you've never met who have a hand in your success. So you might as well be kind to everyone—some of them, especially people in the program, may have packed your parachute.

Your attitude determines your altitude.

SEPTEMBER 4
The Truth about Pinocchio

Most people think that Pinocchio is a children's story about a little boy who kept telling lies until his nose got long. That's not exactly right. Instead, Pinocchio is the story about a boy who kept on telling the truth until he got real.

That's a lot like what we do in the program, isn't it? Keep on telling the truth until we get real? Twelve-Step recovery isn't about flipping a switch that suddenly takes dishonest people and makes them honest. Instead, at least for me, it was a process of progressively becoming less dishonest, as I realized I had less and less to hide. But then, by accepting the unconditional love of my sponsor and others in the program, I found I didn't need to lie to protect myself.

I no longer needed to lie, or at least I started lying a lot less often.

Get real.

SEPTEMBER 5
So What Is Intimacy, Anyway?

*F*or practicing addicts and alcoholics, intimacy just means taking off your clothes in the presence of another human being.

In recovery, intimacy can be defined as "into me, see." In other words, I'm letting you get to know the real me. I'm not hiding, because I'm comfortable enough with myself to let you see me, emotional warts and all.

Here's another definition of intimacy: being yourself with someone else.

How do you achieve intimacy? Tell the truth, and then stop talking, and listen carefully as the other person tells you his or her truth.

Is intimacy really that easily attained?

I would say it's that simple, but I wouldn't say it's that easy. We've been hiding who we were for a long time. One of the benefits of recovery: what you see is what you get.

Come as you are.

SEPTEMBER 6
The Hole in the Street

An addict was walking down the street and fell in a hole.

The next day, the addict went down the same street, tiptoed up to the edge of the hole, and fell in.

The third day, the addict carefully, painstakingly went around the hole, and fell in anyway.

On the fourth day, the addict managed to skirt the hole and get to the other side.

On the fifth day, the addict went down a different street.

What street are you on?

SEPTEMBER 7
Alcoholic Alzheimer's

What's alcoholic Alzheimer's? It's where you forget everything but your resentments.

And here's the chaser…a balanced alcoholic is one with a chip on both shoulders.

The beauty of recovery is that it allows us to lay down the burden of resentments we've been carrying for years, and often for decades. It's amazing how much emotional energy it takes to hate people for long periods of time. It's even more amazing to discover what we can do with that same energy when we free it up for useful purposes. Here's the best definition of resentment that I've heard: *re-sentiment. To feel something, usually negative, again.*

There's a story about two Buddhist monks who come across a naked woman near a stream in a forest. The older monk picks her up and carries her across the stream. An hour later, the younger monk asks, "How could you do that? You're a monk!"

The older monk replies: "I only carried her across a stream. You've been carrying her for three miles!"

You've been carrying people far longer,
and they probably aren't even naked.

SEPTEMBER 8
What the Dickens?

At his seminars and on his audios, master motivator Tony Robbins invites people to do what he calls the "Dickens Pattern." In order to get leverage over yourself to make a change that you need to make, he has you map out on paper, in copious detail, exactly where you will be five years from now, ten years from now, twenty years from now, in terms of your personal relationships, financial situation, and health, if you fail to make necessary changes.

When thousands of people at a convention center are confronting the reality of where their life will go if they don't make the changes they realize they need to make, the emotion, the sobbing, and the tears are absolutely overwhelming.

What about you? What if you don't stay on the path toward sobriety? What will your life look like in five or ten or twenty years? Will you even still be on the planet? Run your own Dickens Pattern and see where you will be if you make the positive changes, and where you will be if you don't. I did it, and the result was powerful.

The future will be here any minute.

SEPTEMBER 9
The Other John Grey

*M*ost of us are familiar with John Gray, author of *Men Are From Mars, Women Are From Venus.* There's another therapist who writes about love and has the same name—albeit with an 'e'—John Grey, author of *Relationship Tools for Positive Change*, one of my favorite books.

In it, Grey speaks of "the hole." He says that when we get angry, a change occurs in our brain chemistry and we cannot think straight, see straight, or talk straight. He calls this a state of going to "the hole." He says that in a relationship, your job is not to allow your partner to drag you to the hole, and it's also your job not to drag your partner to the hole.

It isn't easy, because we are conditioned to respond to the anger of another with our own outrage and anger. To make things worse, in most arguments, after the first couple of exchanges of heated words, the argument stops being about the original subject and starts being about "How can you talk to me that way!"

Well, you won't be talking to him or her that way if you make it your business to stay out of the hole. So make it your goal…to stay out of the hole.

It's a "hole" new world.

SEPTEMBER 10
You Can't Sleep Your Way to the Top

In his classic book, *Awareness*, Jesuit priest and author Anthony de Mello writes of a homeless person in London preparing himself for a night's sleep alongside the River Thames. Just before he drifts off, however, a limousine pulls up and the driver invites him into the back seat, and then chauffeurs him off to an impressive mansion in the center of town. There, a beautiful woman invites him inside, gives him a hot meal, shows him where he can shower and change, and then points him toward a massive, well-appointed bed.

Just as the man starts to fall asleep in that bed, he rolls into the Thames.

You can't sleep your way to the top.

SEPTEMBER 11
It's Not What We Do;
It's What We Leave Undone

*J*ust visited a financial advisor friend of mine at a federal prison where he is doing four years for fraud. While he was drinking, he lost a lot of money for his clients in an investment that had gone bad. He says that if he had just informed them, they would have accepted it, and moved on, because investments involve risk. But he couldn't bring himself to tell the truth, so he created a multimillion-dollar Ponzi scheme that eventually fell apart.

It's not just my friend. For most of us, we get into trouble more often for the things we leave undone than for the things we do. We know we have to pay our taxes, see the dentist, and perform the other basic tasks of adult life. But we don't want to. Or we put things off. As my sponsor, Milton, used to say, "I thought parking tickets were like annuities. You put them in your glove box and they make you money." Not exactly.

Anything you've left undone that you ought to attend to, instead of reading this message?

What are you waiting for?

SEPTEMBER 12
Anyone Who Says "I Feel like a Newcomer" Hasn't Talked to One Lately

When was the last time you spoke to a real, live newcomer? They aren't hard to find. They're the people at your home group you don't recognize, who are typically sitting alone, staring at their cell phones, and trying hard not to get noticed.

Coming to a 12-Step meeting for the first time is a frightening experience. It shouldn't have to be a lonely one. If you see a newcomer, go say hello. If not, will he or she ever come back? If nobody had greeted you, would you have come back?

When I talk to a stranger in a meeting, here are the things I ask: "Is this your home group?" If no, then "Have you been coming a long time?" And if no, "Well how are you doing?"

And then just let them talk. The newcomer needs to talk, because he has probably burned out everybody in his life who might listen to him.

Don't let someone's first meeting
be that person's last meeting.

SEPTEMBER 13
Why Addicts Are Such Great Con Artists

It's because we can actually con ourselves. And the biggest con we run, the biggest lie we tell ourselves, is that our wants are actually our needs—and that we cannot be happy until all those so-called needs are met. What do we want? You name it. Fame, fortune, applause, sex, a new car, a nicer home, a more prestigious job—the list goes on and on, *ad infinitum*.

What are our actual needs? A day of sobriety or abstinence. Our rent or mortgage paid for the month. Enough money in our pockets so that if we die tonight, we would have had enough money for the day. Food and clothing for today only. A bed or couch where we can sleep tonight.

Those are our actual needs. Everything else in life is a want. I'm not saying that those material things I listed are not worth desiring. I am saying that it's silly to commit to being unhappy until we have all of those things. Today will never come back—this is your only shot at it. Are you willing to tie your happiness today to material desires that may not be met in the near future, or perhaps ever? Can you distinguish between desire and a real need?

We're pros at being cons.

SEPTEMBER 14
The Real Money Problem

Most people think that the biggest problem you can have with money is not having any. My Debtors Anonymous sponsor Bob shared with me a surprising fact about wealthy people. In reality, there are people who make plenty of money who are in deeper financial trouble than some people who make almost nothing. That's because those individuals, often addicts and alcoholics like us, keep themselves in a state of vagueness when it comes to their financial affairs. Vagueness is a child-like or even blissful state of having no idea how much money we have, how much we earn, how much is in the bank, how many checks are outstanding, how much we owe on credit cards and student loans, and so on.

Bob calls vagueness the "money drunk." You didn't get clean and sober to keep your financial life in a drunken state. How do you combat vagueness? With a pen and paper. Write down every penny you spend, earn, and owe. Create categories—rent or mortgage, groceries, entertainment, clothing, transportation, personal care, and so on.

Then go over the list with a trusted friend. Just simply seeing the reality of where your money comes from and where it goes attacks the vagueness. You don't need special apps or programs. A humble pen and paper will get it done.

Pay as you go.

SEPTEMBER 15
Go Clean Your Room

I once heard a speaker tape in which the 4th Step was analogized to telling a kid to go clean his room. "If you just say to the kid, 'Go clean your room,'" the speaker began, "we both know nothing's going to happen. Maybe a few things are going to get rearranged.

"But if you instead say to the same kid, 'Go to your room, go through all the toys that you don't want to play with anymore. The toys that are broken, missing parts, are no fun, or you just want to get rid of them because they don't work anymore. Stack them outside your door, and then when you're done, we'll have space for a whole lot of new toys.'

"We both know that the room will end up spotless."

This is how the 4th Step works. It's about getting rid of the toys we don't want to play with anymore. Anger, fear, resentment, manipulation, guilt, and on and on. These are the broken toys we played with or utilized while we were drinking and using. The 4th Step is about stacking them by the door so as to make room for new and better toys. These would include love, patience, tolerance, joy, understanding, and so on.

Time to get rid of those broken toys.

SEPTEMBER 16
You've Got the (Higher) Power

A speaker in Los Angeles named Tom used to say, "No one in Alcoholics Anonymous is any closer to God than the day he or she got sober. And no one in an A.A. meeting is closer to God than anyone else in the meeting. The only difference is in the awareness of the nearness that was there all the time."

It's not as though you have to climb the highest mountain or travel to some distant point to find your Higher Power. It's said that God is both immanent and transcendent—inside us and everywhere, all at the same time. Isn't it time to become aware of that nearness and take advantage of it?

Who knows more about God than you do?

SEPTEMBER 17
Ready to Be Rich

On one of my favorite speaker tapes, the speaker says he would frequently ask his sponsor, "How will I know I'm ready for a big job and lots of money?"

"You'll know you're ready," his sponsor counseled, "when you have them."

The Big Book talks about how we often demand material success even before we have built an appropriate spiritual foundation. Isn't that what we did when we were drinking and using? We would get successful, or lucky, the money would come in, and we'd think it would last forever. Of course, it didn't.

I've also seen cases where individuals received more material success than they could handle because they were still new in the program. They went out, and one never came back, simply because he received too much, too soon.

The Big Book makes clear that spiritual development must precede material success. A.A. experience teaches that this is absolutely the truth.

While you're waiting for your ship to come in,
work on the pier.

SEPTEMBER 18
Here's Your "Round Tuit"

The legendary motivator and speaker Zig Ziglar had a round business card with his contact information on one side and the letters "TUIT" on the other. This was to make fun of the fact that people say, "I'll do it when I get around to it."

Well, his business card was round, and it said "TUIT" on it, making it a round tuit. In other words, no more excuses for doing what needs to be done.

Consider today's message your round TUIT.

So get TUIT.

SEPTEMBER 19
Stop Calling Yourself Names

Like many alcoholics, when I was new, I used to say some pretty terrible things to myself. I would call myself names that I would never let any other human being call me. My first Al-Anon sponsor, Harv, told me what to do about it. He advised, "Any time you use a bad word on yourself, say out loud, 'Thank you for sharing, but I'd rather not be spoken to that way.'"

Harv emphasized that I had to say the words out loud for it to have an effect, and then if I did that for a month or so, I would never call myself by a bad word again as long as I lived.

I did exactly what he said, and it turned out that he was right. I no longer call myself names.

In reality, I am a beautiful child of God, and I never was any of those things that I used to call myself. Today, I know who I am and what I am. So if you're still calling yourself names, try this method. It works.

It just reminds me of the story about the self-important guy in the supermarket who didn't like the service he was getting and told the clerk, "Do you know who I am?" To which the clerk responded by picking up the microphone and announcing to the whole store, "There's a man here in aisle three who doesn't know who he is."

What's the bad word?

SEPTEMBER 20
The Road Is Better Than the Inn

*E*arl Nightingale was the father of the modern personal development movement. On his audio series *Lead The Field*, he quoted Cervantes as saying that "the road is better than the inn." Meaning that we are happier when we are on the path to a meaningful goal than after we have arrived there. Satisfaction, he said, came from the pursuit of a meaningful goal.

The wonderful thing about recovery is that there really is no such thing as arrival. There's no place to get to, just the opportunity to continue to enjoy another day clean and sober. When I got my first-year coin, one of the old-timers told me, "Good. Now you can do it a day at a time like the rest of us." This is why so many people report a letdown feeling after they have gotten their year coin. The sorry few even drink over it.

Keep in mind that the road is better than the inn, and as you approach one goal, start to think about the next one. It's what successful people do.

"Don't look back—something might be gaining on you."
—Satchel Paige

SEPTEMBER 21
Who You Gonna Call?

Sometimes in recovery, we have to make some difficult phone calls—we have to make amends, call creditors, call parole officers, ex-spouses, soon to be ex-spouses, and so on. It's awfully tough to pick up the phone and make those calls. Of course, leaving those tasks undone can have far worse consequences.

The suggestion is to borrow a technique from Debtors Anonymous called "bracketing." In D.A., when you have to call a credit card company or other similar institution, the thought is to reach out first to a fellow member of the program and explain that you've got to make this difficult call.

Then you make the call, and then you call the same program person back and let him or her know that you took care of it. It takes a lot of the fear out of the process, because you don't feel as though you're handling the situation entirely alone.

Bracketing works, and not just for calls to financial institutions. Give it a try.

When you bring your Higher Power on the call,
now it's two against one.

SEPTEMBER 22
You Are in the Efforts Business

The Big Book talks about how few people love success more than alcoholics. It makes sense—we who come into the program with little to no self-esteem tend to stake our entire self-worth on accomplishments rather than on our character.

There's nothing wrong with desiring to succeed. The problem is that you cannot control outcomes, and yet we are staking our emotional, and sometimes even our physical, sobriety, on the outcome of the given situation.

The solution is to remember that we mortals are in the efforts business, while Higher Power is in the results business. It's not our job to try to dictate outcomes. It is our job to put forth our best efforts in any given situation, so that we can lay our head on the pillow at night, feeling proud of our behavior. But since we don't know what's best for us, and we cannot control outcomes, it makes no sense to tie our self-image to results.

The harder you work, the luckier you get.

SEPTEMBER 23
Who Said Work Is a Four-Letter Word?

*M*aybe you don't love your boss, or your job, or your pay. But nothing will change unless you take on the attributes of a "worker among workers," as suggested in this piece of A.A. guidance: Get to work early. While you're there, work hard all day. And just before you leave, say to the boss, "Is there anything else that needs to be done?" And if there is, do it.

If you ask the average employer how many people work for him or her, the honest response will typically be, "About half." In other words, surveys indicate that most workers are disengaged from their jobs. Not us. *The Big Book* says that we actually have a higher earning capacity than most people. We want to make up for lost time.

So if you want to stand out at work, advance, make more money, marry the CEO's son or daughter, and eventually retire to a beautiful farm in Virginia, or whatever, get there early, work hard all day, and just before you leave, say to the boss, "Is there anything else that needs to be done?" And if there is, do it.

Work is a four-letter word, but so is "rich."

SEPTEMBER 24
Still Keeping Your Options Open?

Addicts and alcoholics love to keep their options open. It gives us a sense of control, freedom, and choice. In reality, "keeping your options open" is code for "never getting anything done." At some point, you've got to choose a place to live, a career path, a spouse or a partner. What are you waiting for?

I'm not suggesting that you rush into anything—that's addictive behavior. But so is procrastination, which is also a trait of addicts and alcoholics. At some point, we have to make commitments. Initially, of course, to sobriety, and eventually, to relationships, career, and community.

At some point, we have to get out of the stands and onto the field. Can't do that if we're failing to commit. Not sure if you're ready? Ask your sponsor. He or she will most likely have an opinion on the subject.

Keeping your options open
usually means "I have no life."

SEPTEMBER 25
That's All, Folks!

An out-of-work voiceover actor visited the reception desk at Warner Bros. every week for a year, always asking the same question: "Got any work for me?"

Fifty-one times, that out of work actor, hardly a rare species in Hollywood, was turned away.

On the fifty-second week, the receptionist said, "Well, they need a voice for this rabbit for a cartoon. I don't think it's going to amount to much."

The rabbit was Bugs Bunny, and the out-of-work actor was Mel Blanc, who not only created the voice of Bugs Bunny, but also those of Daffy Duck, Yosemite Sam, Foghorn Leghorn, and a host of other voices familiar to children of all ages.

Imagine if he'd stopped asking after fifty-one weeks. Someone else would have gotten the job, and Bugs Bunny—and our childhoods—would have never been the same.

The miracle begins in five minutes.

SEPTEMBER 26
Start Where You Are

In the late 19th century, a Philadelphia man named Russell Conwell felt directed to start a new university in order to honor his Higher Power. In order to fund the university, he went on the lecture circuit, delivering a talk called Acres of Diamonds thousands of times. With the money he earned, he founded Temple University.

Acres of Diamonds tells the story of a farmer in Africa who left his farm to seek his fortune elsewhere, looking for diamonds. Eventually, he ran out of money and had to sell his farm. The buyer noticed some shiny stones at the bottom of a creek that ran through the property. Of course, they were diamonds. The moral of the story: You don't have to pull "a geographic" or move somewhere you've never lived in order to succeed. Start where you are, and let success come to you.

Don't just do something, stand there.

SEPTEMBER 27
You Don't Get What You Deserve in Life

That sounds like a shocking statement, but if you think about it, it's true. Instead, most of us get what we think we deserve. If we think we deserve to succeed, then that success mindset triggers us to take the actions that lead to success. If we think we are destined to fail—if we believe failure is what we deserve—then that's what we get.

I used to do a jail panel with my friend Jerry D. He would ask the inmates, "How many of you have parents who told you that you would end up in jail one day?"

Nearly all hands would go up, every single time.

Sometimes we have to overcome a lot of negative conditioning from childhood. But the important thing is to raise our "deserve level"—my friend Gary Kadi wrote a book about how to do just that. You don't get what you deserve—you get what you think you deserve.

If we got what we really deserved...

SEPTEMBER 28
When Addicts Move

Addicts and alcoholics always think that life is going to be better somewhere else, with someone else, doing something else. We are convinced that we can move, change jobs, find a different relationship, get rich, or whatever, and *then* we will be happy.

The challenge is that if we do move, then we have to "start over" in the program. This doesn't mean that we have to reset our day counts. It does mean that we have to find new meetings, make new clean and sober friends, and so on. The challenge is that wherever you go, they will do things differently from the way they did the program where you used to live. And we have a tendency to think that the way we do things where we got sober is the right way—because that's the way that saved our life.

Sometimes the best thing an alcoholic can do, when confronted with the urge to leave town and live somewhere else, is to lie down until the feeling passes.

Is this move necessary?

SEPTEMBER 29
Meditation: The Real Payoff

People in recovery meditate because the 11th Step suggests it. We go into meditation seeking many different things—the ability to hear our Higher Power more clearly, peace of mind, whatever. For me, the biggest benefit to meditation is the fact that I can hear, at least for the ten minutes a day that I put into my practice, something other than the endless chatter in my brain, much of which is deeply, comically, and pathetically negative.

When I meditate, I can hear the sound of my own breath. I can hear birds chirping, traffic sounds, or the hum of the refrigerator. All of these sounds remind me that there is something else in the world other than my own mind chattering away. If that were the only benefit of meditation, for me, that would be enough.

It's bad enough that we produce an endless stream of negative chatter; it's even worse that we actually listen to it and believe it.

Peace, be still.

SEPTEMBER 30
Don't Turn Genetics into a Death Sentence

Genetics may be the least understood branch of science because most of us think that our genes dictate your destiny. In fact, in most cases, they don't. Your genes point to a predisposition for addiction or other illnesses. Someone who has a predisposition for alcoholism yet never takes a drink is not going to become an alcoholic.

Most of us interpret genetics as the elimination of any sense of free will. "I have to be this way, because that's my genetics." That's not true. Genetics might point in a certain direction, but you have the power to make life choices that dictate how your life actually turns out.

Motivator Tony Robbins points out that modeling is as important, or more important, than genetics. When your alcoholic parent was stressed, he or she reached for the bottle. That modeling made a deep imprint on you, so that's what you did. Genetics might have pointed you in a direction but modeling carried you there.

Recovery is a supermodel.

OCTOBER 1
Your Parents Did the Best They Could

*O*ne of the biggest blessings I learned in Al-Anon came when a speaker said, "Your parents did not wake up every morning saying, 'How can I mess up little Jimmy's life today?' Instead, they did the best they could with the tools they had. The purpose of Al-Anon is to give you better tools, so that you can do a better job."

Exactly! Maybe your parents didn't do a great job. They must have done some things right, because here you are. Instead of writing them nasty, scolding letters, or cutting them out of our lives, let's honor and respect them for the things they did well. And if we receive shortcomings in their parenting styles, let's try to do a better job with our own kids. And for God's sake, let's not label our parents with terms like "toxic" or "dysfunctional." Let's try to find the humanity in our parents, instead of giving them way too much power at this stage of our lives.

Your parents must have done something right.

OCTOBER 2
The Helper's High

We're all familiar with the runner's high, the feeling of wellness our internal chemistry set produces when we get in a strenuous workout or a long run. There's a short-term runner's high and even a long-term version, where you feel good on a regular basis because you work out regularly.

Fascinatingly, there's also a "helper's high," and it has the same short-term and long-term causes and benefits. This shows that just as we are wired to move, we are wired to help one another. As my late sponsor Milton's A.A. business card read, "God divided man into men that they might help each other."

Help someone else…and get high.

OCTOBER 3
Claiming My Seat

Back to Basics founder Wally P. describes 12-Step discussion meetings as "group therapy without a therapist." This isn't just useless; it's dangerous. When people are talking about serious emotional issues, but they don't have anyone to guide them or help them make sense of what they're talking about, they're often worse off than if they hadn't brought them up at all.

Twelve-Step meetings were never meant to be group therapy. Their real purpose is to allow the clean and sober member to carry a message of experience, strength, and hope to the newcomer. The newcomer couldn't care less about your relationship problems, how much you hate your boss, or the fact that you lost your cat. There's nothing more selfish than going to a meeting and ignoring the fact that newcomers are present and they need to know how the 12 Steps will work for them.

Take your mess to your sponsor
and your message to the meeting.

OCTOBER 4
Beyond Right and Wrong

As a practicing alcoholic, I was extremely judgmental. Things were either right or wrong, and most of the time, they were wrong. Of course, that was simply my negative self-image reflecting outward. Now that I've been sober for a while, I don't see the world in such black and white terms. I've moved, for the most part, from a world of right and wrong to a world of comfortable and uncomfortable. I'm either comfortable or uncomfortable with a situation, and if I'm uncomfortable, it's up to me to determine why.

It's a lot easier to go through life when I'm not judging everyone and everything, and usually judging them negatively.

How would I know what's right and what's wrong?

OCTOBER 5
People a Lot Busier Than You Are Going to Lots of Meetings

I always laugh when I hear people say that they're "too busy" to go to a meeting. I'm married, have four young kids, run a business with forty employees, work out regularly, do marathons, sing in choruses, and do a bunch of other cool stuff. I also have time for three to four meetings a week, in addition to regular contact with my sponsor, my sponsees, and my Higher Power.

If you're too busy to go to meetings, your priorities are out of whack, because anything you put ahead of your program, you will lose.

Don't let the things that recovery gives you...
take you out of recovery.

OCTOBER 6
When We Call Our Sponsors, We're Doing Them a Favor

*N*ewcomers often say in meetings that they're afraid to call their sponsors because they're afraid of disturbing them. In fact, sponsors are delighted when their sponsees call. It's a chance for us to get out of our obsessions, resentments, and overall negativity, and instead, help you with your situation. I'm convinced that if most sponsees knew how nuts their sponsors still are, even after decades of clean time, they would run in horror from the program. But that's our little secret, isn't it!

---

*I call my sponsor even when I have no issues to talk about—
I call it "testing the hotline."*

OCTOBER 7
If You're New, You Have More to Offer Than You Think

Sometimes people in their first weeks or months of sobriety believe that they have next to nothing to offer those who are newer to the program than they are. That's really not true. The "new newcomer" trusts and can relate to someone with a few weeks or months far more readily than someone with decades of sobriety.

They tell a story about the newcomer who turned to the person on his left in the meeting and said, "How much time do you have?" "Ten years," the person replied. The newcomer turned to the person on his right. "How much time do you have?" "Ten days," the person replied.

"Ten days!" the newcomer exclaimed. "How did you do it?"

If you know how to read a meeting book and explain it to the newcomer, you have plenty to share.

Who can you help?

OCTOBER 8
My Most Valuable Possession
Doesn't Fit in a Safe-Deposit Box

It isn't a house, a car, or a fancy watch. Instead, it's the memory of my last drink to date.

I know just who I was with (an ex-girlfriend), where I was (her apartment), and exactly what I wanted from her. I also remember the miserable feeling I had when I experienced a moment of clarity in my car outside her apartment when I suddenly realized what an animal I had become.

I never want to be that person again.

The memory of your last drink or use to date becomes your most valuable possession, because it reminds you of the you that you don't ever want to be again. Where were you, and what were you doing? It's also a great thing to share, because it helps the newcomer identify.

If you can't recall your last drink or use to date,
you may not have had it yet.

☕

OCTOBER 9
Get a Job

*M*y sponsor Milton used to say that he was never surprised when an alcoholic gets sober, but he was surprised when an alcoholic would get a job.

The suggestion, when you're new, is to get what the old-timers called a "sobriety job." This is a job not necessarily in your own field, or the kind of job your education level would point you to. Instead, since many of us were out of work for a long time before we entered the program, getting a job reminds us that our time is so valuable to others that they're even willing to pay us to stick around and do stuff for them.

I have a law degree from one of the top law schools in the United States, but when I got sober, I found a job temping for seven dollars an hour. The job put a few dollars in my pocket, raised my self-esteem, and kept me out of trouble. Since it was part-time, I was still able to make nine meetings a week for my first two years.

They call it a "sobriety job" because it's not what you'll be doing for the rest of your life. It's just something to tide you over as you make your start in recovery.

Your raise becomes effective the moment you do.

OCTOBER 10
The Three-Second Rule

In S.L.A.A.—Sex and Love Addicts Anonymous—there is a suggestion called the "Three Second Rule." This means that if you see a person of the sex to which you are attracted, opposite or same, you train yourself only to look directly at them for a maximum of three seconds.

First, staring at people makes them uncomfortable, so it's something we shouldn't do. Second, all we're doing is driving ourselves crazy, because it's highly unlikely that the person we're staring at—on the sidewalk, in a meeting, at work, or in a restaurant—is going to drop everything and run to be at our side.

Psychologist Terry Gorski tells of the time he offered his therapist his definition of the perfect woman.

To which the therapist replied: "Terry, what on Earth would someone like that want with you?"

Rim shot.

Look, but don't stare.

OCTOBER 11
Aim for the Pillow Sober

When I was new, I heard a few key suggestions: when you get up in the morning, hit your knees and ask your Higher Power for a day of sobriety. Then figure out what meeting you're going to that day, and plan the rest of your day around the meeting, instead of the other way around. Put A.A. (or your own 12-Step program) in the number-one slot. At night, as a courtesy, hit your knees again and thank your Higher Power for a day clean and sober.

Remember that your business is going to meetings, and everything that happens outside of meetings is none of your business. That's pretty much still how I live my life twenty-seven years later.

When you stick to the basics,
you never have to go back to basics.

OCTOBER 12
How to Choose a Sponsor

The suggestion is "find someone with something you want." It might be serenity, it might be material things, it might be a hot girlfriend or boyfriend, or a cool car. Whatever.

I'll share with you how I found my first A.A. sponsor. About five years before I got sober, I heard a voice—yes I was hearing voices—after a particularly brutal argument with a girlfriend. The voice said, "I love you and I will never leave you."

Five years later, after I'd gotten sober, I was driving to a meeting. I said to my Higher Power, "I want to pick a sponsor at today's meeting. Please give me a sign."

I was listening to various men share, and then one said, "And I was at my lowest moment when I heard a voice saying, 'I love you and I will never leave you.'"

His name was Hal R. He sponsored me for my first two years of sobriety, and he gave me the program I still follow today.

I still get goosebumps thinking about that "coincidence."

The key to benefiting from sponsorship is having one.

OCTOBER 13
"It Can't Happen to Me."

When I was in my first year of sobriety, there was a lot of talk in my home group about a fellow many of the guys knew. He had woken up in county jail one morning, having killed someone with his car in a blackout the night before. He had no recollection of his car crossing the yellow line and killing the person, but he was still looking at twenty-three years in state prison, of which he ultimately served seventeen.

Sometimes you hear it said in meetings that "You can't scare an alcoholic or addict," but this man's story scared the heck out of all of us. Of course, this was a room full of sober men. So maybe the expression should be, "You can't scare a *practicing* alcoholic or addict." Why not? Because when we're still using we say, "That can't happen to me, and the proof is, that never happened to me."

Anything that can happen to any alcoholic or addict can happen to any of us. And just because something never happened to us doesn't mean we're somehow immune.

There's a first time for everything,
even for things you never dreamt could happen to you.

OCTOBER 14
Putting the Puzzle Back Together

Around my first sober birthday, I sat next to a guy at a meeting who had gotten sober in prison. In fact, this was his first meeting on the outside. I asked him what he heard at A.A. meetings behind the walls that had the most effect on him.

He told me a story about a man who wanted to watch a football game on TV, but his little son wanted to play. So the man took a map of the world from the newspaper, tore it into pieces, and told the son, "Here's a puzzle you can do." He figured he'd be able to watch at least half of the game that way. Ten minutes later, the son pointed with pride to the puzzle, which was complete.

"How did you do it so quickly?" the father asked, amazed.

"On the back of the puzzle, there was a picture of a man," the boy explained. "And when you put the man back together, this world comes together."

The good news is that you didn't have to go to prison to hear that story, and neither did I.

Pick up the pieces.

OCTOBER 15
I'll Give You One Good Reason for Getting Drunk

There are tons of excuses for drinking—getting fired, getting dumped, getting a new girlfriend or boyfriend, getting a new job, getting a speeding ticket, or even getting looked at funny on the bus. Ultimately, all of these situations are just excuses for drinking and using.

There's only one reason why addicts and alcoholics drink and use—it's because we're addicts and alcoholics, and that's what we do.

Sobriety, then, is an unnatural act. One of the cornerstones of sobriety is getting honest about everything, but especially about the nature of our disease. We cannot drink or use in safety. If we do pick up, it's because we are addicts and alcoholics, not because outside situations caused us to do so.

No one ever forced a drink down my throat. The same is almost certainly true for you.

So let's distinguish between excuses for drinking and using, on the one hand, and reasons for picking up. And again, there's only one reason for picking up—it's because that's what alcoholics and addicts who don't have a strong program, do.

Don't lie to yourself.

OCTOBER 16
The More You Know, the More It Means

I have no idea how my fascination with A.A.'s early history developed. Most people in recovery are familiar with the story of how Bill W. and Dr. Bob met and developed what became Alcoholics Anonymous, the granddaddy of all 12-Step programs. I found that the more I learned about A.A.'s early history, the more A.A. meant to me. When you think about it, it's incredibly unlikely that these two individuals could possibly have connected as they did, and that a movement could have resulted.

I read the A.A. conference approved biographies of Bill and Bob, and then other things like *What Is The Oxford Group?*, Wally P.'s books, and a variety of other books about how A.A. formed.

The more you know about the unlikely nature of the program's existence, the more you value it. At least that's how it was for me.

What do you know?

OCTOBER 17
We Have a Wrench for Every Nut

They say that if you like all of the people at all of your meetings, you probably don't go to enough meetings.

The reality is that not every speaker at every meeting will say something that you consider meaningful or useful. Eventually, you may well come to the point that everyone in the meeting is speaking from a different corner of your heart. But initially, some people will make sense to you and some won't.

This is why it's so important to try a variety of meetings and find your own particular "flavor" of recovery that suits you best. The perfect sponsor for me may well be a lousy choice for you. The good news is that there's so much variety in terms of the way alcoholism and addiction manifest themselves in the people who attend meetings that you are almost certain to find someone who speaks your language.

Walk where we walk, so you don't blow up.

OCTOBER 18
No, That's Not Happening

A member commented wistfully, "I wish I could trade my odometer for my net worth," meaning that his car mileage was high and his bank account was low.

Sitting in a meeting and expecting that the fairy godmother of recovery is going to strike you rich with her magic wand is, alas, not an option. Somehow we think that all we have to do is go to meetings and everything will magically fall into place in our lives.

That's just not true.

As it says at the end of the 9th Step promises, these great things will happen..."as long as we work for them."

Am I willing to work for the things I want, or do I still have an overly developed sense of entitlement? When will I recognize that the world owes me nothing?

Only an addict expects a reward for accepting a gift.

OCTOBER 19
If You're So Happy, Tell Your Face

The *Big Book of Alcoholics Anonymous* tells us that "we absolutely insist on enjoying life" and that in sobriety we are "happy, joyous, free," and that "we are not a glum lot." It sounds good, but have you been to a 12-Step meeting lately? Could anyone look more glum than a bunch of clean and sober people?

Sometimes it seems that members go out of their way to hide whatever happiness or joy they have out of sight of other members. You would think that a room full of people bound by the great news that they no longer have to drink, use, eat, or abuse people or other substances should be the happiest group of people you've ever seen.

You'd be wrong.

The next time you walk into your home group, look around and ask yourself, "Are we an attraction, a group of people whose gratitude and relief stretches from steerage to the captain's table?"

If you're so happy, tell your face.

OCTOBER 20
Is Our Program Simple or Selfish?

Sometimes you hear people say, "The 12 Steps is a simple program for complicated people."

To which my sponsor Milton would rejoin, "No—it's a simple program for people who think they're complicated."

The longer I've been clean and sober, the simpler my life has gotten. I no longer have to remember which lie I told. I no longer have to figure out how I'm going to pay the Mastercard bill with a cash advance from American Express. I no longer have to figure out what I'm going to do for work or where I'm going to live, because I've been fired or thrown out of a relationship one more time.

Life doesn't necessarily get easier—being married, raising children, running a business, and all the other things we do in our abstinent, sober lives, also have complications. But they are a heck of a lot easier to handle than the jackpots I kept on getting into back in the day.

No, it isn't. Drinking and using is a selfish program. It means that we are putting our need to obliterate reality ahead of the needs of everyone else in our lives—family, coworkers, neighbors, friends.

That's selfish.

In fact, recovery isn't a selfish program—it is a self-caring program.

Simple doesn't always mean easy, but it's a lot more fun.

OCTOBER 21
Our Unofficial Marriage Manual Comes from Our Traditions

*I*f you love irony, as I do, it probably strikes you as entertaining that a serial philanderer, Bill W., wrote *The Big Book* chapter "To Wives." He also hadn't held a real job in years, but that didn't stop him from writing "To Employers." And despite the fact that he never had children, he still wrote a chapter called "The Family Afterward."

The good news is that Bill did provide us with a great guide for relationships—A.A.'s 12 Traditions.

It's hard to have a relationship go wrong if the common welfare of the couple comes first, or if both parties are committed to being emotionally self-sufficient. And it certainly strengthens a marriage or relationship if the parties are not constantly debating their opinions on outside issues.

So, Bill, we know you meant well with *The Big Book*, but when it comes to relationships, you really got it right with the Traditions.

Take my advice—I'm not using it.

OCTOBER 22
If Recovery Were Easy, Everyone Would Be Sober

My sponsor Charlie says that he'd like to find the guy who said that life would be easy, take him into the alley, and beat the you-know-what out of him. Life *isn't* easy. One of the harder things to do, in fact, is get clean and sober. And yet, lots of people leave the program, because they think it's just too hard. Going to meetings, being personally responsible for your behavior, not drinking or using—you've gotta be kidding me! You have to do all that?

When I was new, I heard in a meeting, "If someone tells you the program is easy, run!"

It's not easy because we are reversing years or even decades of thinking and acting. We're developing a relationship with a Higher Power, unlike anything we've ever sought. We are opening up ourselves to people whose last names we don't even know. And above all, we are giving up our best friend and most trusted ally, alcohol, drugs, or whatever your activity or substance of choice might be.

It does get easier, but let's face the fact—early sobriety is hard.

Hang in there.

OCTOBER 23
Is It OK to Pray for Parking Spaces?

*I*f you really want to get eyes rolling in an A.A. meeting, announce from the podium that you pray, successfully, for parking spaces.

You can count on some big blowhard to get up and crosstalk, reminding you that we don't pray strictly for our own ends—or at least that's what *The Big Book* says.

In point of fact, you can pray for anything you please, from a parking space to a new job to the Cleveland Indians winning the World Series. (Good luck.)

But if you are going to pray for a parking space, why not pray for a parking space not just for yourself but for the guy behind you who also needs one? It couldn't hurt.

Now that you're sober, it's not just about you anymore.

OCTOBER 24
The Greatest Gift

I met my Debtors Anonymous sponsor, Bob, on January 31, 1994, at a meeting on a sub-freezing winter night in New England. The temperature did not keep Bob from standing outside the meeting with me for a full twenty-five minutes, to explain how that program worked. He didn't just tell me what to do—he listened to my situation with a sense of compassion and focus that I found both loving and, honestly, thrilling.

And that's how it's been for twenty-five years. When I speak, Bob actually listens. Active listening is the greatest gift that you can give another human being. You cannot get it on Amazon or buy it used on eBay. All it takes is the intention to focus on what the other person is saying.

Most of the time, we don't do this. Instead, we listen to the beginning of what the other person says and we think of our response and simply wait for the other person to stop talking, so we can offer our brilliant rejoinder. Or, worse, they start talking, and we go into a trance state, our thoughts drifting back to our own lives, concerns, and even obsessions.

Not Bob. For twenty-five years and counting, Bob has given me the greatest gift any human being could offer. He listens. He even listens to my phone messages.

No greater love.

OCTOBER 25
Everybody's Negative, Not Just Us

A lot of alcoholics and addicts think that the negativity their minds generate on a seemingly constant basis is a function of their disease. So they're confused that the negativity doesn't go away once they put some clean time together. In fact, the human mind naturally tends toward the negative. This isn't a function of addiction or alcoholism—it's just human nature.

The person who made this observation is Napoleon Hill, in his classic work, *Think and Grow Rich*. Hill says that human beings are governed by fears, which must be overcome, because as long as we dwell on those fears, our minds grow naturally toward the negative.

Your life is probably better than you think. Unless there's physical violence in your home, in which case the Al-Anon fellowship suggests that you remove yourself and any children immediately, everything else has a solution. You can always get a job, you can always work out terms on the money you owe, judges take a very positive view of defendants who are working a solid A.A. program, and people will forgive you for a lot of your bad behavior.

When it comes to negativity—just say no.

OCTOBER 26
A 12-Step Approach to Time Management

Alcoholics and addicts love to get tons of things done. The more we move about, and the faster our pace, the less we have to look inside. So we love being busy. The problem is that sometimes we end up focusing on the wrong things, or because we're trying to get so much done, we wear ourselves out, or we are late to appointments, dates, work, doctor appointments, and so on.

So here's the 12-Step secret of time management: *Do one less thing every day.*

The Big Book talks about how smart it is to pace ourselves so that we do not burn out or waste our energy foolishly. One practical way to put that guidance into effect is to commit to doing one less thing every day. By lightening your load, suddenly you have time for everything else. And when you're able to spend some time thinking about your own self, instead of running in circles, you end up spending your time and energy much more wisely.

Just because you're busy, doesn't mean you're effective.

OCTOBER 27
Your Number Is Up

*I*n his classic work, *The Art of Loving*, psychologist Erich Fromm wrote that people tend to put a number on themselves, a number based on their attractiveness, economic status, education, material possessions, and so on.

In other words, we are spiritual beings who have turned ourselves into economic objects, and we only tend to consider ourselves appealing to people who have less or the same overall "score."

The reality is that we are not economic objects—we are beautiful children of God, and there is absolutely no way to reduce that wonderful news to a number.

Instead, we need to remember that not everything that counts can be counted, and that not everything that's counted counts.

Don't sell yourself short.

OCTOBER 28
"May My Dog Smell You?"

When I was newly sober and fairly broke, I needed a share of an apartment because I could no longer afford the condo I had bought a few years earlier. I followed up on one such opportunity and a kindly, older lady—I would imagine she was in her early sixties—met me at the door. "Could I have my dog smell you?" she asked. "My dog has really good judgment."

So I let her dog smell me, and I apparently passed the test because she offered me the share of the apartment, but I turned it down. At that moment, my life wasn't worth very much, but it just seemed sad to me that a person had so little faith in her own judgment, especially by that point in life.

Sometimes people say, "I came to A.A. and stopped drinking, so I'm all set." Maybe they are, but I needed a lot more out of recovery than a share of an apartment and a job. I needed better judgment. Fortunately, I got it.

I may not know what's best for me,
but my sponsor thinks he knows.

OCTOBER 29
We Try to Solve in Public
What We Can't Solve in Private

The founders of Herbalife and Core Power Yoga have remarkable similarities in their life stories. Both founded incredibly successful international companies that help countless people improve their health and well-being every day. Both lived in fabulous multimillion-dollar Southern California beach homes. Both men were worth tens of millions of dollars at the time of their deaths.

And both men were found dead in their beautiful, multimillion-dollar beach homes, one with a needle in his arm and the other with a toxic level of alcohol in his bloodstream.

All too often, we try to solve in public what we cannot solve in private.

It's great that Core Power Yoga and Herbalife exist, because of all the people those entities serve (and employ, for that matter).

Wouldn't it have been better if the founders could also have done the simple thing that 12-Step recovery asks of each of us? Namely, save your own life before you save the world.

If you're going to be the Messiah, don't make a mess.

OCTOBER 30
I'll Do Anything, as Long as It Isn't Inconvenient

Alcoholics and addicts are funny people. In our minds, we will scale the highest mountain or descend to the bottom of the deepest sea if it would please our partners. But we sure don't want to do the dishes.

We just love big, grandiose gestures, especially those that attract a lot of attention. On the other hand, man, how we hate to be inconvenienced. Get out of bed, go to the drugstore and get something for your partner, spouse, or newborn child? But it's so late!

Go to a meeting? Don't you realize how hard I worked today?

Sobriety is inconvenient. A.A.'s co-founder Dr. Bob once described recovering from alcoholism this way: It's a cold, wet night, you've just gotten in from work, you've got dry clothes on and you're sitting by the fire, opening a good book...and suddenly the phone rings.

I know it's inconvenient, but answer the call.

OCTOBER 31
The Terror-Movie Marathon

Around Halloween, there's nothing better than watching a marathon of scary movies. Puts you right in the mood for the holiday. The problem with alcoholics and addicts is that we love to show ourselves scary movies all day long, even when Halloween is months away. No wonder we're scared all the time. So if you want to stop being scared, stop showing yourself scary movies.

Alcoholics and addicts, even when clean and sober, are famous for "catastrophizing"—imagining a situation as turning out for the worst, no matter how likely or unlikely such a worst-case scenario might really be.

When you find yourself showing yourself a scary movie, remember that you have the power to turn it off and watch something else. Did you realize that on your phone or other device, you could watch thousands of hours of comedy on YouTube?

Maybe get yourself laughing the next time you start terrorizing yourself. Scary movies are great for Halloween. For the rest of the year, they're definitely not what you want to watch inside the privacy of your own brain.

What else is on?

NOVEMBER 1
The Good News about Fear

Yes, there is good news. I wasted so much time in early sobriety, and even in sobriety that was not so early, afraid of what my feelings would be like if something happened or didn't happen. In other words, nothing had happened yet, but I was still sitting in fear of what might happen. Or what might not happen. In other words, I was afraid of my own feelings.

There's a fine line between ignoring one's feelings, which I did throughout my drinking days, and paying far too much attention to them—giving them too much power over my actions and my life, generally. There's actually good news about fear, though. In *The Gift Of Fear*, security consultant Gavin de Becker points out that anything that you're afraid of *isn't actually happening now and may never happen.*

So it takes some retraining of our thinking to accept this idea, but it's powerful when we do. The next time you find yourself projecting anxiously into the future about something that may never even become reality, remind yourself that fear is proof that whatever you're afraid of isn't happening right now.

Feelings aren't facts, although they sure feel like facts.

NOVEMBER 2
Just Stop Trying

If you've ever said, "I'll try," it means that there's no way on Earth you're going to do it.

"Will you swing by my party tonight?"

"I'll try."

"Will you be at the meeting tomorrow morning?'

"I'll try."

Stop lying to yourself and other people—"I'll try" means that you've made up your mind that you're not going to do it, whatever it is.

To prove this point, try to pick up a pencil from the floor. I'll wait.

No—don't pick it up, just *try* to pick it up. It's impossible, right? Right.

Stop trying and start doing.

NOVEMBER 3
What If That Was Your Last Haircut?

A friend in medical school brought me, one Saturday night long ago, into the lab where twenty dead bodies lay on twenty tables, so that the students could study anatomy with them. The first body I saw, which, I must admit, was the only body I looked at, was that of a male in his early seventies. He looked like a pleasant, friendly guy, and what I remember most was that he had a nice haircut. I wondered for a long time what he would have done differently had he known that the haircut he had just received would be his last.

Would he have lived his final day any differently? Made different choices?

What about you—what if you knew that you had just gotten your last haircut? What would you do differently? And if you would make those changes, why wait?

Human beings are the only creatures, as far as we know, with an awareness of their own mortality. Instead of fearing death, let's use our awareness of the limited time we have on Earth to our best advantage.

We're not here for a long time,
but we are here for a good time.

NOVEMBER 4
It's Murder, I Tell You

*G*erry Spence is one of America's most famous defense attorneys for individuals charged with murder. In his autobiography, he wrote that whenever he addressed the jury for the first time, he would always confess his nervousness.

First, it was shrewd—the life of his client hung on how well he could make his case. In addition, confessing his fears humanized him in front of the jury, who might otherwise have seen him as a big-shot defense attorney.

I've followed Spence's lead on many occasions in my work, telling people that I'm a little bit afraid because I want to do a good job. No one's ever criticized or condemned me for that little bit of honesty. It turns out that when you tell people the truth about you, instead of trying to hide, which is what I always had done when I was drinking, they like you more. Who knew?

Tell the truth—people might just like you for it.

NOVEMBER 5
Character Defects...or Just Bad Habits?

*M*y late, great sponsor, Milton D., never really liked the phrase "character defects." His attitude was that most of the things that the program describes as character defects are actually just bad habits, and you can replace a bad habit by recognizing it and then replacing it with a better habit.

When you think about it, his approach makes sense. Fear? A bad habit. Manipulation, resentment, anger, rage, envy, and so on? All bad habits. This approach empowers us to eliminate these behaviors right away, right now, today. We can just try to do better right now.

It's not as though we'll never get angry or resentful or fearful again as long as we live. The good news is that we don't have to give in to the unpleasant feelings, get loaded, and get behind the wheel. The better news is that we have more control over our words and actions than we realize. So we don't have to make others suffer just because we are unhappy. That's a bad habit, too. We can't "work on our character defects." What we can do is ask for help, pray for patience and tolerance, and try to replace bad habits with better ones.

You've got the power.

NOVEMBER 6
"My Name Is Charlie B., and I'm an Alcoholic."

In a wonderful Peanuts cartoon, Charlie Brown says, "I've developed a new philosophy—I only dread one day at a time."

I guess for Charlie Brown, that represents progress—prior to that he had been dreading entire weeks, months, or years at a time. When you think about it, that's what addicts do. We tell a story that our future's going to be no better than our present or past, and then we make that story a reality.

In truth, in recovery, your past has nothing to do with your future. I've known some very wealthy people with long-term contented sobriety. You would never know…

I've known people who were complete failures at relationships who became happily married once they became clean and sober. Bad parents become better parents. The unemployable become successful employees. It's really amazing what happens once we put down the drink, the drug, or the substitute.

Your past has nothing to do with your future—
that's why they call it the past.

NOVEMBER 7
Are You an "Adult Child"? Time to Pick One

The very first 12-Step meeting I attended was an Al-Anon meeting with an "adult children of alcoholics" focus. I was so blown away by the reality of forty different people telling stories about *my* childhood, which they happened to live in their own homes growing up, that I could barely get out of bed the next day.

I went back to the same meeting the following Tuesday, and the Tuesday after that and the Tuesday after that. There was no mention of recovery or Steps. Instead, people just kept telling the same stories about how miserable their childhoods were.

I don't mean to throw an entire program under the bus, because I'm sure there are some terrific A.C.O.A. meetings out there. But I do have my doubts about adult children of alcoholics. At some point, we have to decide whether we want to define ourselves as adults, which means that we are responsible for our choices and actions, or children, which means that it's still mommy and daddy's fault.

It's very hard to become an adult if you're marinating in blame. The last thing you want to do is to be part of a group that encourages such immature thinking.

Time to grow up.

NOVEMBER 8
Your Feelings Are Perfect...

Your feelings are perfect, which means that no one has the right to criticize them. No one has the right to say, "You shouldn't be afraid," or "You should be happy."

At the same time, while our feelings may be perfect because they are ours, they're not always an accurate representation of reality.

It's a delicate balance the program teaches between feeling our feelings and giving them too much power. No one has the right to criticize your feelings, including you. But at the same time, since feelings aren't facts, you may find it more comfortable to reside in a world of facts, because the facts are usually pretty promising, especially the more that you stay clean and sober.

You no longer need have thoughts about your thoughts
or feelings about your feelings.

NOVEMBER 9
Fear Is the Ultimate Energy Suck

I had no idea how depressed I was until I started going to meetings and feeling good in the meetings. That provided me with a sharp contrast at what I felt the rest of the time, which was pretty miserable. Little by little, I began to feel just as good outside meetings as I did inside them. That was a nice change.

Similarly, with fear, I had no way of understanding just how much time I spent locked up in fear until I got to the program and learned the basics of faith. People say that fear and faith cannot coexist at the same time, but that was not true for me. I was perfectly capable of being afraid and having faith at the same time. Eventually, faith came to outweigh fear. I'm hardly serene, but I'm reasonably happy most of the time, which is a pretty good deal for an alcoholic.

Less fear, more energy.

NOVEMBER 10
We Are Always Repeating Scenes

*N*ot to get too psychological on you, but one of the biggest truths I learned outside the 12-Step world was that we are forever recreating scenes…until we resolve them. For example, if we had a parent who didn't listen, we just keep going out there finding other people who don't listen, because we have to keep recreating that scene.

We stop recreating scenes when we learn to tell the truth about what happened, process them with a capable authority, and move on.

That capable person might be your sponsor, a therapist, a religious leader—anyone you trust who's capable of helping you with this. Until we stop repeating scenes, we tend to blame the new people in our lives, the people of whom we are recreating those past scenes, and nothing comes to us. In reality, we've nobody but ourselves to blame, because we are choosing not to come to terms with the reality of whatever happened long ago.

What does the director say if the scene is going badly? Cut!

NOVEMBER 11
"If I Drink, Will You Sponsor Me?"

One day after our lunch meeting, my late, great sponsor Milton D. sidled up to me. "You have such a great program, Mike," he said. "If I ever drink again, would you sponsor me?"

You've got to understand that Milton was an icon in our circles in sobriety. When he spoke in a meeting, everyone leaned forward to listen, like in those old E.F. Hutton ads. One day, years later, I told another one of Milton's sponsees what Milton had told me.

He just shook his head and laughed.

"Mike," he said, "he says that to all of us."

I was devastated.

Bottom line: Milton never drank. He had well over forty years when he passed, so none of us needed to sponsor him.

Still, it's a really cool thing to tell your sponsees.

NOVEMBER 12
Sought through Prayer, Meditation, and Exercise...

I once heard someone say in a meeting, "If they were writing the 11th Step today, they would say, sought through prayer, meditation, and exercise...'"

That sounds about right to me.

The way the founders of Alcoholics Anonymous understood prayer and meditation, prayer was when you spoke to God and meditation, which we might call contemplation today, was where you went quiet and listened to see what God had to say to you.

It's a lot easier to stay sober and remain in conscious contact with a Higher Power if you're healthy. It's a lot easier to stay healthy if you get out and get exercise. This might mean just going for a long walk every day, or it might mean doing Ironman Triathlons. Or anything in between. It's not too late to undo the damage we've done to our bodies through years of excess and abuse. Your body is a lot more resilient than you may give it credit for.

You've got to pay for better health—it's just that you can buy it today at the gym and the supermarket or try to buy it later, for a much higher price, at the doctor's office.

Use it or lose it.

NOVEMBER 13
There's No Such Thing as an Original Sin

That comes from an old Elvis Costello song, and he was right. It's remarkable how people in 12-Step programs are deathly afraid of doing the 4th Step, because they don't want to learn the truth about themselves.

The truth that the 4th Step reveals is that the alcoholics and addicts are just like everybody else on the planet. We get angry. We get fearful. We get resentful. We manipulate. We do things we aren't proud of.

The only difference between us and "civilians" or "normies" is that we do these bad things a lot more often than regular people. But when we do get angry and frustrated, we don't just pace around and blow off steam, or whatever normal people do. Instead, we get a 12-pack and then we get behind the wheel.

I always tell my sponsees, "If we discover a character defect that you have that I've never heard of before, I'll get them to name a Step after you." It's never happened. We are all interchangeable beneath the skin, which is the reason why 12-Step programs work so well. We understand each other.

You may be special, but you're not unique.

NOVEMBER 14
The A.A.A. of Love

*O*ften, addicts and alcoholics don't know how to behave in a love relationship that excludes drugs and alcohol. Well, if you call Triple A to get your car out of a ditch, call on this A.A.A. to make sure your relationship is on the right road. And here it is: Attention, Affection, and Appreciation.

Attention means simply to look your partner in the eye when he or she talks. Put down the phone and be fully present. *Affection* means to study your partner and figure out what means the most, whether it's touch, words, or gifts. *Appreciation* means don't take anything for granted—thank constantly, with words you speak and with little notes, like a Post-It note on the steering wheel.

Don't wait for a breakdown to call <u>this</u> A.A.A.

NOVEMBER 15
A Program for People Who Talk Too Much

I'm thinking about starting a new 12-Step program for people in meetings who talk too much. I'm going to call it "On and On."

They say that we learn patience and tolerance from those who use the meeting as an opportunity to check in, complain, hit on newcomers, and the like. Truth be told, at one morning meeting I attended regularly, my regular seat was next to the door that led out to the men's room. That way, I could make a quick escape if certain people were called on.

We are not saints.

Silence isn't just golden—it's fabulous.

NOVEMBER 16
You Don't Have to Have
a Heart Attack over It

In the book *Type A Behavior and Your Heart*, two San Francisco cardiologists, Meyer Friedman and Ray Rosenman, first used the term "Type A" to describe their hard-driving patients who had bought themselves a heart attack as a reward for all their aggressiveness.

The doctors' unusual prescription for their patients was to reclaim lost parts of their personalities through the appreciation of beauty. They were told to go to a park (this was way before cell phones) and just admire nature. Or go to a museum and look at the paintings and sculpture, or go to a concert hall and listen to a symphony.

It's pretty good advice for us addicts and alcoholics, because when we are focused primarily on our addictions, our world gets awfully small and dark. Who knows—you might end up liking culture and nature more than you thought.

I'd rather have an art attack than a heart attack.

NOVEMBER 17
Stay with the Basics and You Won't Have to Go Back to Basics

Twelve-Step programs are pretty simple, once you get the hang of it. Trust God, clean house, help others—any questions? If you haven't begun to take the Steps, then just focus on the slogans—live and let live, turn over, think.

And then after you go through the Steps, you'll find that living clean and sober goes back to living the slogans.

When I was new, they told me to ask God to direct my thoughts and actions, and then to hit my knees at night as a courtesy to say thank you for a day without substances.

Or to put it even more simply: Are you willing to give up one thing so that you can have everything, or are you willing to give up everything, so that you can continue with that one thing?

Keep it simple.

NOVEMBER 18
Humility Versus Humiliation

The words humility and humiliation get confused, but they mean two completely different things. Both words come from the Latin word *humus*, meaning "from the earth" or "grounded." Humility means "to be grounded," which is what sobriety gives us, and humiliation is to be driven into the ground, which is what addiction does to us.

Most people seem to think that humility means denying that we're special or good at something or that we worked hard to stay sober. In an Al-Anon pamphlet on the 12 Steps, Lois, writing about Step 7, provides a better explanation. Humility, she writes, means seeing myself as I am. What are we? We are beautiful children of God. We aren't perfect, but life isn't a game of perfect.

My sponsor, Milton D., liked to say that an A.A. group gave one of its members an award for his humility. When he accepted it, they took it away.

Stay grounded, my friends.

NOVEMBER 19
What I Do Now Is What I Did Then

When I was new in sobriety, it seemed that every old-timer would use those exact words when he or she celebrated an A.A. birthday. I love the formulation because it's so simple and clear. Nine little words explaining that there really is no such thing as an advanced degree or black belt in 12-Step recovery. The same "basics" keep us going as we move into long-term sobriety.

The great motivator, Earl Nightingale, tells the story of a ship captain sitting at a restaurant at a port. If you went up to him and asked him, he could tell you exactly how he would get to the next port, even though he had never been there, and even though he would not see land for 95% of the journey.

The answer: the ship captain would do the same simple things every day, with confidence that they would take him to his destination.

It's the same thing for us. The same simple actions that we take in our first ninety days of sobriety are equally effective in our ninth year, our nineteenth year, or at any time.

If you start your day on your knees,
life cannot drive you to your knees.

NOVEMBER 20
No, You Don't Have a "Broken Picker"

Sometimes you hear people make light of their repeated relationship failures by saying that they have a "broken picker"—they just pick the wrong people.

Which is another way of saying that everything is the other person's fault.

Sorry. You don't have a broken picker. You're just lousy at relationships.

I speak from considerable experience. When I was drinking, I brought out the worst in every woman I ever dated. It's amazing how badly a relationship goes when you lie a lot, get angry over nothing, get inexplicably moody, and sometimes get drunk and stupid in front of her parents.

Relationships can be very different in sobriety, but we will never be attracted to, or attractive to, anyone at a different spiritual level from where we are. If you want to have a better relationship, be a better partner.

As Terry Gorski says, "If your relationship sucks, so do you."

NOVEMBER 21
The Real Goal in Al-Anon

The real goal in Al-Anon is not to get a drinker to stop drinking. Instead, it's to get to a point where *your opinion of me has no bearing on my opinion of me.* When you grow up in an alcoholic home, as I did, there's a good chance that you were essentially trained to have your level of self-esteem dictated by others. How ironic—self-esteem implies that the self should do the esteeming! Not your parents, your boss, your love interest…but you, yourself.

So how do we make that shift? How do we get to a point where your opinion of me has no bearing on my opinion of me. First and foremost, we take the Steps, because as Bill W. points out in the *12 and 12,* "If I have a relationship with a Higher Power, I don't let other people play God to me." Beyond that, if we want high self-esteem, we do estimable things. (There's no such word as esteemable.)

In other words, the more positive actions you take, the better you'll feel about yourself. So stop wishing for a better childhood or parents who are not alcoholics and instead ask yourself, what estimable, positive actions can I take today?

I'd like you to like me,
but if you don't, I'll be fine.

NOVEMBER 22
Born to Lose

*E*arl Nightingale, whom I quote frequently in these pages, tells the story of a tattoo artist who says that one of his most requested designs is the words "Born to lose." When asked why so many people choose such a negative expression, he replies, "Before tattooed on skin, it's tattooed on mind."

Sometimes people say that all you need to get out of a 12-Step program is physical sobriety. If that's all we stick around for, we will miss out on the spiritual growth that will allow those negative words tattooed on our minds to fade away. The good news is that erasing a mental tattoo is a lot less painful than erasing a physical one!

What does your tattoo say?

NOVEMBER 23
The Last Laugh

A famous comedian in one of my Los Angeles home groups told a story about getting bounced from The Tonight Show because he appeared drunk one night. He said that after he got sober, he got an invitation to perform on Beverly Hills public access television. He accepted, and said that he was full of self-pity as he drove over to the studio, because not all that long ago, he was appearing on The Tonight Show, and now? Local cable access.

Of course, Beverly Hills cable access is a little different from similar setups across the country. One of his viewers that night happened to be the same producer of The Tonight Show who had booted him years earlier.

The producer called. "You look different," he said.

"I got sober," the comedian replied.

"I thought so. Want to come back on The Tonight Show?"

The moral of the story: If you're invited to show up somewhere sober, show up. You never know where it might lead.

Now, <u>that's</u> comedy!

NOVEMBER 24
You Can Add to My Life,
but You Cannot Subtract from It

In Al-Anon, one of the character defects that the program discusses is "giving away the power." This means that we are allowing another person, typically one of those alcoholics we see or hear so much about, to take the reins in the relationship and dominate us.

Chuck C., whose A.A. retreat talks were collected in the volume, *A New Pair Of Glasses*, says that "You can add to my life, but you cannot subtract from it," meaning that you can enhance my life and I welcome that. But I will not give you permission to take away my serenity, my peace of mind, or anything else.

That would be "giving away the power," and that would be something we don't want to do.

Addition, yes; subtraction, no.

NOVEMBER 25
Take the Label off Thanksgiving, and It Magically Becomes...Thursday

Some members of Alcoholics Anonymous insist that they were top shelf drinkers, at least for the first hour of any given drinking session. After that, they didn't really care what they put in their systems, as long as it kept them happily drunk. Some of our members were wine connoisseurs (of course), with collections of hundreds or even thousands of fine bottles of wine in their specially-built wine cellars.

At the end of the day, though, whether it's a terrific bottle of wine or vodka you buy by the liter, and always in a different drugstore every day, so that no one suspects you're an alcoholic, if you take the label off, they're all just plain alcohol. Nothing more, nothing less.

The wise course with Thanksgiving is to take the label off that day and remember that another name for Thanksgiving is Thursday. We don't drink on Thursdays, and we don't drink on Thanksgiving. Even if it fell on a Friday, which it doesn't.

Don't let the fancy label fool you.
Booze is booze, and Thanksgiving is Thursday.

NOVEMBER 26
Your Brain for Sale: $100,000!

The great motivator Zig Ziglar used to tell audiences, "I wish I could sell all of you your brains for one hundred thousand dollars. Then, you would appreciate your brains…and I would have one hundred thousand dollars!"

Ol' Zig was on to something. We tend only to appreciate things we pay for. This is why so many people come to 12-Step programs and have little regard for what goes on. Why? Because it's free.

You might say, "But what about all those expensive recovery houses?" And my response would be that typically the addict is not the one who writes the check—it's the parent, the spouse, insurance, or the employee assistance plan. One of the challenges, therefore, of entering into a 12-Step program is respecting it, even though it doesn't cost anything.

And by the way, never say, "I earned my seat" in a given 12-Step program. No, you didn't. You received that seat by the grace of your loving Higher Power. Just because you drank or used a lot doesn't mean you earned it.

If we really valued what we had, we wouldn't spend
so much time envying what the other person has.

NOVEMBER 27
Stop Playing God

One of the most powerful themes in the *12 and 12*, one to which Bill W. returns on three different occasions in that book, is the concept of right relations. Bill writes that practicing alcoholics don't know how to have healthy relationships with other people. Instead, they either try to dominate other people or they depend on them to an unhealthy degree.

Bill adds that at some point, the people we dominate get sick of us and flee, and the people we depend on get tired of us and also depart, leaving us alone yet again. His solution: developing a healthy relationship with a Higher Power. When we have a healthy relationship with a Higher Power, he writes, we don't need to play God to our fellows, nor do we let them play God to us.

So the road to having healthy relationships with people is first having a healthy relationship with God.

What do you call a practicing addict or
alcoholic without a girlfriend? Homeless.

NOVEMBER 28
This One Thing Makes Stopping Drinking and Using Look Easy

Living sober requires alcoholics and addicts to do the one thing they find harder than anything else. I don't mean giving up drugs and alcohol, or overeating or inappropriate relationships. The bigger challenge is to stop running the universe.

Sometimes we think that by getting sober, we have a shield against any sort of bad thing ever happening to us again as long as we live. That's not true. We can still have health issues, money issues, relationship issues, or all the other challenges of life, normal and abnormal. The difference is that, by the grace of our Higher Power, we don't have to drink or use over them.

That's why it's so important for me to take my sponsor's suggestion and start my day by hitting my knees. It's an act of humility that reminds me that I'm not running the show. It also allows me to "rejoin" Alcoholics Anonymous by reminding myself, and my Higher Power, that I am an alcoholic and I need to be kept from the first drink for the first day. It also reminds me to take life on life's terms. As Chuck C., a long time Southern California A.A. member, wrote in *A New Pair Of Glasses*, "God is a gentleman. He doesn't go where he isn't invited."

Spirituality is like vitamin C—it goes right through you,
and you need another dose the next morning.

NOVEMBER 29
Why Is Having a Higher Power like Chicken Soup?

Is it possible to stay sober without having taken the 2nd and 3rd Steps, without having invited a Higher Power into your life? It's possible, but it's much harder that way. It's bad enough to sponsor yourself, but to be your own Higher Power as well? Doesn't that sound like the recipe for disaster?

Here's why: The alcoholic mind is capable of holding two contradictory thoughts at the same time. One is, "I cannot drink or use in safety." The other is, "This time it will be OK."

As long as my mind cannot keep me sober, I need something bigger, more powerful, to do the job. That's why I have a Higher Power.

It's not ideal to sponsor yourself. It's disastrous to be your own Higher Power.

All you have to know about God is that you aren't it.

NOVEMBER 30
Giving—I Mean, Pointing—the Finger

I'm not talking about *giving* the finger. I'm talking about *pointing* the finger of blame at someone else.

In Al-Anon, we say that "when you point one finger at someone else, three fingers are pointing right back at you." In other words, the exact same shortcoming you are noticing in another person is something that you must have—otherwise you would have been incapable of noticing it in your friend.

If you're blaming the other person for anger, look at your own anger. If you're blaming the other person for being manipulative, check out your own manipulative tendencies. And so on down the line. This is why, after more than thirty years of Al-Anon, I no longer point the finger when I am upset with someone because I don't want those three fingers pointing back at me.

Instead, I use my whole hand.

What's my part in this situation?

DECEMBER 1
Who Invented Boozy Office Parties, Anyway?

Office parties are tamer than they were in the *Mad Men* era, but there's still plenty of booze flowing, which means there's plenty of opportunity for the guy in IT to have a few belts too many and say something he shouldn't say to Mary from Accounting. So who invented boozy office parties anyway? If you're fortunate enough to have employment and your company does office parties, the only question you need to ask yourself is whether you really need to go. If it's a heavy drinking party, no one will miss you. And whether you're there or not, probably no one will even care. Alas, we're just not that important or memorable.

If you do go, follow this tried and true piece of A.A. lore—go to the bar immediately upon arrival, get a soda, a juice, or a glass of water, and carry that drink with you wherever you go. If you are carrying a drink, other people are less likely to ask, "Why aren't you drinking?" And if you put the drink down even for a microsecond, you have to go back to the bar and start all over, because that drink is no longer your drink. We alcoholics love to pick up the wrong drink "accidentally on purpose," taste that alcohol, and then say, "Oh, well. I blew it. Time to get loaded." Better still, maybe just stay home this year. Especially if you have a crush on Mary in Accounting.

The party's over…

DECEMBER 2
Sobriety—What's in It for You?

The minimum you will receive if you follow the suggestions in your 12-Step program is physical sobriety. The maximum is serenity. And in between, you can have anything you want and work for.

The most amazing things happen when people stay sober, all of which point out the primary truth that "your future has nothing to do with your past." People who were failures at relationships suddenly… OK, not suddenly, but over time, develop the ability to function well as part of a couple or family. Children forgive their boozing and carousing parents (maybe not immediately, but eventually). People who couldn't or wouldn't work get jobs. People with jobs get big careers. People whose careers had been in the toilet rocket to the tops of their fields.

Just remember that in order to achieve all these wonderful goals, the relevant Big Book chapter title is "Into Action"—not "Into Thinking." You cannot think yourself into right action, but you can act yourself into right thinking. You cannot think yourself into success unless you are also willing to work hard for what you want.

Take what you like, but pay for it.

DECEMBER 3
Nobody "Gets" Sober

Sometimes you hear in meetings, "I just can't get sober." Or, when members are gossiping about other members, "He just can't get the program." Let's get real. The program isn't something you *get*. It's something you *do*. When we mistakenly think of the program as something you get, that adds a level of hocus pocus or magic or chance or even unfairness for the process. In reality, the universe does not play favorites—it doesn't give a head start in recovery to this person while throwing unfair obstacles in the path of another.

Every day, there are choices that recovering addicts and alcoholics must make if they are to maintain their sobriety or abstinence. Clean and sober people look at the menu of sober actions and take most, if not all, of them. They ask for help. They develop a relationship with their Higher Power. They pray and meditate. They talk to their sponsors. They read the literature. They go to meetings. They return calls from fellow members of their 12-Step groups. They are of service. And so on.

Don't delude yourself into thinking that there's something wrong with you because you haven't been able to "get" the program. You probably just haven't done the things that are necessary. Do the necessary things, and you'll get it.

It doesn't say "Half measures availed us half."

DECEMBER 4
The Best Way to Stop Eating Sugar Is to Stop Eating Sugar

I have a sponsee in A.A. who goes in and out; sometimes it feels as though he's out more than he's in. I empathize because I struggled mightily with sugar and white flour. When the going gets tough, the tough overeat. Or at least that's my M.O.

It's amazing how much weight you can gain from overeating *healthy* snacks. We have four kids, so I say I don't live in a crack house…I live in a cracker house.

I'd love to tell you that I've had years off of sugar and white flour, but that's just not the case. So when it comes to getting off and staying off of these two forms of poison, one day I decided, *enough.* When I hit my knees in the morning to "rejoin A.A." and turn my will and my life back over to my Higher Power, I also ask to be kept from white sugar and white flour. Works like a charm.

The waste is a terrible thing to mind.

DECEMBER 5
The Single Most Ignored Suggestion in 12-Step Recovery, Especially by Newcomers Who Are Single

*D*on't date in your first year.

We've all heard it, but how many people have actually followed that suggestion?

Newly recovered alcoholics and addicts are terrified of being alone. Of course, we don't want boyfriends or girlfriends—we want hostages. Psychologist and author Terry Gorski says that we want to keep people around who can blow our minds on demand like cocaine. That's because the most successful love relationship we who are children of alcoholics saw was the love of our alcoholic parent for his or her favorite kind of alcohol or drug.

The trouble with dating in your first year is that this is a time when you really need to focus on yourself. Sure, the sex may be great, but remember that nobody ever died of loneliness (or from lack of sleep, for that matter). Worse, the high highs and low lows of a new relationship, especially with a person as crazy as oneself, is often enough to drive a newcomer back to alcohol or drugs.

Give it a rest.

DECEMBER 6
I Never Thought I Was Enough

When I was in kindergarten at East Hills School in Roslyn, New York, they took us into the sixth-grade classroom, for whatever reason, to show us what was in store.

I took one look at those desks and I edged over to my teacher, Mrs. Stannard.

"I'm never going to be big enough to fit in those desks," I anxiously explained. "What do I do?"

I'm not enough of a scholar about human psychology to know whether my anxiety as a five-year-old put me on a path toward alcoholism, or whether anxiety is simply part of the human condition. I do know, however, that addicts and alcoholics find emotions like anxiety and fear so unbearable that we have to bury those feelings under copious amounts of alcohol, drugs, sugar, sex, or what have you.

Feelings are like dynamite—the more you tamp them down, the bigger the eventual explosion. If you're feeling anxious, call your sponsor or go to a meeting. If you're not feeling anxious, call your sponsor or go to a meeting.

By the time I got to sixth grade,
I fit in the desk just fine.

DECEMBER 7
Is Anger a Character Defect?

In the *12 and 12*, Bill writes that God gave us instincts for a reason. Anger is an instinctive reaction, so it can't be all bad. It's really just a question of what we do with the anger that dictates whether we're turning it into a negative or positive. So the question arises: In what sense could anger be considered a positive?

Anger is a desire for change. When we're angry, it's because there are situations in our minds, our homes, our workplace, our community, our country, or our world that we think are wrong. If nobody got angry, nothing would ever get better. So anger in and of itself is not a character defect. It's just a question of what we do with the anger we feel that dictates whether we're using this basic instinct in a positive or negative way.

If I transformed my anger into a desire to get sober, or to improve my marriage, or an effort to foster change on a societal level, that's good. If I use my anger as a way of terrifying or controlling others so they do things my way, that's not good.

Anger is not a character defect, contrary to popular opinion. It's what we do with our anger that dictates whether we are operating on that instinct in a healthy or unhealthy manner.

No one can "make" you angry—only you, yourself.

DECEMBER 8
Adult Children Just Look Young

Why do adult children look so young?

Here's a fascinating tidbit about adult children of alcoholics, according to recovery author Janet Woititz: ACOAs tend to look younger, dress in a more youthful fashion, and groom themselves to appear younger than do other people in society. They're doing so, according to Woititz, because they're hoping that by remaining forever young, mommy and daddy will come back and all will be well.

That's actually quite sad when you think about it. It's unfortunate to invest all that time and energy in seeking an outcome that almost certainly will not happen. Mommy and daddy aren't coming back.

The good news is that you do not need the approval, the friendship, or even the love of a parent in order to have a happy life as an adult. There's nothing wrong with looking nice, and there's nothing wrong with looking young, especially in a youth-oriented society like ours. But do that because you want to do that. Don't do it because you think that if you keep yourself looking like a child, mommy and daddy will come back.

Don't confuse desires (parental love) with needs
(maturity, sobriety, abstinence).

DECEMBER 9
What Does a Good Son or Daughter Do?

When I was five years sober, my sponsor Milton asked me how things were with my mother. "Not great," I admitted. "We got into it again."

Keep in mind I was thirty-nine at the time. By that point, I had been through tons of therapy and inventory writing, but I still hadn't been able to get to a healthy place with my mother. After all, as the expression goes, she knew how to push my buttons…because she installed them.

"Take out a piece of paper," my sponsor growled, in that voice that said, *This isn't a suggestion, this is an order.* "Write on it, 'What Does A Good Son Do?' And then make a list of all the things that a good son does. He calls. He sends a card. He remembers birthdays. He sends a gift. He visits. He sends flowers. Then, anytime you feel the slightest bit of rage toward your mother, take out that list, which you'll keep in your wallet, and do one thing on it."

From that moment to this, I have not experienced a single moment of rage toward my mother, who passed away recently at the age of eighty-two.

It's hard to be a real adult if you're still mixing it up with mom and dad.

DECEMBER 10
Are You _Feeling_ Your Feelings
Or _Being_ Your Feelings?

There's a great line in the movie *City Slickers:* "If hate were people, I would be China."

We give our emotions authority to hijack our brains and eliminate any common sense or rationality from the way we think. It's great to be in touch with your emotions, and that's actually one of the gifts of recovery. The problem is when we let emotions drive the bus and dictate what we think, say, and do.

Don't get me wrong—I'm not talking about ignoring your emotions. I am suggesting that there's a critical difference between feeling our feelings, which typically means that our feelings are in charge, and of simply noticing our feelings.

Even the difference in the way we speak about this can have a calming influence on ourselves. As in the difference between, "I am angry" and "I am noticing anger." In other words, it's wise to have a little bit of distance between ourselves and our emotions. Otherwise, when we see red, we turn into a charging bull. When that happens, nobody wins.

Noticing your emotions, instead of being them,
has a soothing effect.

DECEMBER 11
It Says Don't Judge, but It Also Says Stick with the Winners

It seems like a contradiction—the program suggests that we give up being judgmental. At the same time, we are exhorted to "stick with the winners," meaning that we're supposed to identify the people in the program who are successful role models for our sobriety, and then stick with them. So how can we identify those people…if we aren't judging?

Typically, when we judge, we condemn. It seems as though it's inherent in human nature to run the other guy or gal down so as to increase our own fragile self-esteem. Maybe this is just a trait of alcoholics and addicts, but I don't think so.

So when we say don't judge, what we really mean is, don't condemn. Don't find fault with your neighbor just to make yourself feel good about yourself. Some people are further down that path toward love and service than others. It's smart to identify those people and be with them as much as we can, so that we can see how they live life and manage their sobriety.

Winners live and let live.

DECEMBER 12
Are 12-Step Programs Cults?

It might look that way, with all the dopey chiming in, and things like "Hear, hear!" and "If He were sought," and everybody saying "Hi, so-and-so" after people introduce themselves as alcoholics or addicts.

But no, 12-Step programs are not cults. If they were, why would we wait until newcomers had lost everything to get ahold of them? Most cults want to make a lot of money off of their followers. By contrast, 12-Step programs wait until you've lost the house, the bank account, and the cars. We wait until you have next to nothing. *Then* we want you to join. For proof, the next time you're in a meeting, count the newcomers. Try to guess how much money they're worth collectively, and then divide that amount among the rest of the people in the room. That's really not an efficient way to run a cult, is it?

Similarly, most cults have a "special place" they want you to go to, where they can indoctrinate you and make you sign long-term contracts. Our idea of "long-term" is…twenty-four hours. And in terms of having a special place, most A.A.s have never been to Akron, Ohio where the fellowship was founded, or to Bill's birthplace in New Hampshire.

If A.A. is supposed to be a cult, it's doing a lousy job.

DECEMBER 13
What Earthly Good Is Prayer?

It depends whom you ask. Some people will tell you that prayer can change the world, restore people to health, help people get new jobs, get parking spaces, and so on. Others will tell you that the purpose of prayer is to give human beings the opportunity to speak to their Creator, without necessarily looking for some specific outcome as a result of the encounter.

So whether you believe prayer gets you cash and prizes or just a few moments of quiet reflection, that's fine. The twelve traditions of Alcoholics Anonymous and every other 12-Step program state that "we have no opinion on outside issues." The purpose, methodology, usefulness, and benefits of prayer are a matter that each member gets to decide for himself or herself.

In A.A., we explain prayer as "speaking to God," while meditation is "listening to God." God's always there, and we can say or ask anything. That's the beauty of the spiritual freedom that 12-Step programs teach. You can literally say anything to your Higher Power, and it's OK. I'm not aware of any other religion or spiritual practice that gives the members so much freedom.

If your God cannot handle your anger, get a bigger God.

DECEMBER 14
Will You Marry Me? (Limit: Five)

*I*n *Getting the Love You Want,* relationship expert and author, Harville Hendrix, asked a fascinating question: Out of all the thousands and thousands of people we meet in our lifetimes, why is it that we are attracted enough to only a tiny number of them to want to marry them?

Hendrix suggests that as we grow up, the way our opposite sex parent treated us creates a template in our brains that dictates how we expect to be treated by a relationship partner when we are adults. If we were treated lovingly and kindly, then we create a template in our minds that screens for those people and screens out everyone else. If we were emotionally abused by our opposite sex parents, then only people who are emotionally abusive get through the door.

The good news, he writes, is that we can change the template, so that we are attracted to, and attractive to, people who are healthier than what our initial template might have offered us. This kind of change doesn't happen overnight. Yet one more reason not to date (or at least date seriously) when we are newly sober before we have allowed this transformation to happen within us.

In relationships, water finds its own level.

DECEMBER 15
No Complaints for Three Weeks, Please

In his book, *A Complaint Free World*, Will Bowen challenges readers to go three weeks without complaining about anything. And anything actually means everything—other people, work, politics, the weather, you name it.

Bowen says that it takes the average person four to six months to accumulate those twenty-one straight complaint-free days. He recommends wearing a wristband that we move to the opposite wrist every time we complain. The practice of going complaint free is an amazing way to retrain one's mind. If a brain generates complaints, but then we aren't willing to share them with the world, eventually the brain just gets sick of the whole thing and stops complaining.

It's a friendlier way to go through life. It took me about four or five months to make it through three weeks without complaining. I think I'm a lot happier for having taken the challenge.

You might just end up happier,
which is nothing to complain about.

DECEMBER 16
What It Takes to Start a New Meeting

Resentment and a coffee pot are all you need. Sometimes people feel unhappy with his or her home group. Maybe the group doesn't focus enough on recovery and it feels like cocktail party chatter instead of recovery. Or maybe there are some blowhards who persist in telling other people what to do. Some folks will go out and start a new meeting. There's nothing wrong with this—whatever the underlying motivation, now there's a new group, and it will prove convenient and appropriate for some folks who might not have liked the prior group.

Starting a group is extremely easy. You file a simple form with the central office, call around to various churches or other facilities to find a location, make an agreement, and then start talking it up. It may take a while before a meeting catches on, but it's very satisfying when it does.

One thing I'm not a fan of is announcements along the lines of, "The Tuesday such-and-such group needs your support." If a meeting is no longer serving, it's time to change the format or shut it down. No use propping something up that no longer benefits people.

Meeting makers make meetings,
and meeting starters benefit everyone.

DECEMBER 17
R.E.L.A.T.I.O.N.S.H.I.P.

Twelve-Step programs are famous for their acronyms. H.A.L.T. means *Hungry, Angry, Lonely, and Tired.* F.E.A.R. means, among other things, *Face Everything And Recover.* T.I.M.E. stands for *Things I Must Earn.* And so on.

But my all-time favorite 12-Step acronym comes from a movie star who was a part of my home group in Santa Monica, California. One day, prior to the meeting, he took me aside and shared this one with me. I tried not to make a big deal out of the fact that there were so many stars in the meetings—they needed their anonymity. But I won't lie. This was kind of a fun moment for me.

Ready?

R.E.L.A.T.I.O.N.S.H.I.P.—*Really Exciting Love Affair Turns Into Outrageous Nightmare. Sobriety Hangs In Peril.* Truer words were never spoken.

If you're in Al-Anon, just change *sobriety* to *serenity,* and it will work for you, too.

S.O.B.E.R. = Son Of a B****, Everything's Real!

DECEMBER 18
You Can't Get in Trouble for What You're Thinking

My sponsor Milton told us that he was never comfortable with any religious doctrine that punished you for what you thought. First of all, you cannot really control your thoughts—anything can come into your mind. You can choose what thoughts you entertain, but it's not fair to punish people for things that are beyond their control.

Second, Milton said, the whole point of having free will was to decide whether or not you were going to act on a particular thought. And in life, you can think anything you want, but people only judge you for what you do and what you say.

The difference between a thought and an obsession is that a thought is something you have, while an obsession is something that has you. So you want to be careful about what repetitive thinking you allow yourself to get into, because eventually, you'll act on the idea behind it. But in the meantime, whatever you may be thinking about your boss, spouse, kids, or that loudmouth guy in the group always criticizing *The Big Book*, if you don't say anything, you cannot get in trouble.

You don't say!

DECEMBER 19
How Can I Be So Smart and So Stupid at the Same Time?

This is a question I asked myself frequently in my drinking days. I'm not a stupid person, and I'm hardly an uneducated person. I graduated from one of America's most selective private colleges and from one of the top law schools in the United States.

I like to say that I overcame every advantage on my way to the bottom.

For a smart guy, I made a lot of dumb choices. Displaying a bad attitude at work. Bringing out the worst in, and unceremoniously dumping, every woman foolish enough to invest her heart with me. Making a commitment to being broke—at least it looks like that's what I did, when you look at my financial track record during my drinking years. I have no idea how I survived.

And then I got sober.

As one of my sober friends says, "I read the dumb book, I went to the dumb meetings, I listened to my dumb sponsor, I took the dumb Steps, I said the dumb prayers, and I got really, really smart."

Funny how not drinking and using raises your IQ.

DECEMBER 20
Don't Just Do Something; Sit There

Sometimes newly recovering alcoholics and addicts get into heated rush thinking about making up for lost time. It's easy to understand why. I threw away about seventeen years of my life on alcohol, although all that drinking seemed like a good idea at the time. Once I got sober, I wanted to make up for all of those losses in the blink of an eye, or at least by my first birthday.

The biggest danger is to put material expectations and demands ahead of the program. I've seen people work extremely hard at rebuilding their careers and finances in their first year, to the exclusion of actually working a solid program. In their cases, that first year stretched on for multiple years, because everything they put ahead of their recovery, they lost.

It may seem as though your life is over when you come in, but in reality, as Joe and Charlie point out in their *Big Book Comes Alive* presentations, we alcoholics and addicts get to lead two lives—the drinking one and the sober one.

As it says in the Al-Anon book, *One Day At a Time*, slow motion gets you there faster.

Get a (second) life.

DECEMBER 21
No, You Can't Figure It Out

Alcoholics and addicts often have an overly developed belief in their own abilities to "figure it out" no matter what "it" is. How to get sober. How to get a job. How to find a new romantic partner. How to…well, the list goes on ad infinitum. In all fairness, many of us grew up in homes where there was no help, where our parents were so detached from our emotional needs that we literally had to figure everything out ourselves. Old habits die hard, but now it's time to adopt a new one—asking for help.

The "big three" of A.A. suggests are, of course, don't drink, go to meetings, and ask for help. Don't drink and go to meetings? It's easy to understand why those things made the final cut. But asking for help? Is that really so vital to a recovering person's success?

You better believe it. If you ever hear yourself saying, "I've got to figure it out," hit the pause button. Most of the time, we're trying to figure out things that are way beyond our own experience or knowledge base. This is why God created other people, especially sponsors and mentors. The good news is you don't have to figure out much of anything at this point. Find people you trust, ask them for help, and watch how much smoother your life gets.

Figuring it out is buying life experience retail;
asking for help is getting it wholesale.

DECEMBER 22
Are You the Life of the Party?

When we're drinking and using, we love parties, partiers, and partying. Free alcohol and drugs? Potential new romantic interests? What's not to like?

But then we get clean and sober, and all of a sudden, the idea of parties becomes a drag. Why exactly would I want to hang around other people who are drinking and using if I cannot? Why do I want to go to a family or business event that is likely to be boring?

A.A.'s answer: ask not what the party can do for you, but ask what you can bring to the party. How can you contribute? I don't mean financially, I mean what can you bring to the party that will make it better to all? You can bring a positive attitude. You can bring your ability to listen instead of to dominate conversations. You can bring your desire to understand people and see what makes them tick. These are all great ways to ensure that you have a great time at pretty much any party…and, even more important, that you get invited back.

"In America, you can always find a party.
In Russia, Party always finds you."
—*Yakov Smirnoff*

DECEMBER 23
The Miracle Begins in Five Minutes

Is impatience a feature or a bug? The good thing about impatience is that it causes us to act. The bad thing is it sometimes causes us to take irrational acts or get frustrated when things don't go our way as soon as we think they should. When I was fairly new in Al-Anon, I used to have a running argument with my second sponsor, a wonderful woman named Jan. She would say, "In God's time," to which I would respond, "God's time is now!"

She was right and I was wrong.

For most of us, who are used to having our minds blown or our feelings altered instantly by drugs, alcohol, sugar, sex, spending, or some other substance or behavior, recovery unspools at an unbearably slow rate. This is why so many people say, "If this is as good as it gets, I'm outta here!"—which, of course, is never true.

It's understandable to want things now. But sometimes it's best to just let things unfold in God's time instead of our time. What's the rush?

The miracle now begins in four minutes.

DECEMBER 24
Declare a Major in Recovery

There are certain suggestions that make enormous sense for any recovering addict or alcoholic to follow. Go to meetings regularly. Choose—and use—a sponsor. Take the Steps. Read the literature. Help others. And so on. Beyond the basics, it seems that the people whose sobriety I admire the most have "declared a major" in recovery. Some of them fall in love with doing hospitals and institutions work. Or they serve beyond the group level as G.S.R.'s. Or they represent their Districts.

Others like to start meetings, and it's very satisfying when the meetings they start take hold, grow, and become an integral part of recovery in their community. Some others major in sponsorship. They have the time and the personality that allows them to serve multiple sponsees. Perhaps they are retired and have a lot of wisdom and life experience to go along with the time.

Isn't it time for you to start asking what you can do for others, once you're solidly on your own path?

What's your major?

DECEMBER 25
You Can Either Wait for Santa, or Be Santa

Addicts and alcoholics love Santa Claus because he gives us exactly what we like best—something for nothing. If there were ever a group of people who loved free stuff, it would be us. But on Christmas Day, now that we're sober, we have choices. We can be miserable and mired in thoughts of unhappy Christmases of the past, or we can put on our Santa hat and go out there and bring some joy to someone else. Once again, we stand at the crossroads of miserable, self-pitying, and eventually loaded...or happy, joyous, and free.

The holiday season presents innumerable opportunities for us to share joy with those who have less. Can you go to the store and buy a bunch of stuff and bring it to a homeless shelter? Can you show up at an alcathon even though you "don't need a meeting right now," find a newcomer who looks really down and out, and give him or her twenty bucks?

There are millions of people in need, which means there are millions of ways to be Santa.

Instead of wondering what's under your tree, why not go out and put a few things under the trees of other people? Your gift may be the only one they receive this year.

There's always somebody worse off than you,
and that person isn't all that hard to find.

DECEMBER 26
If You Treat Everyone as If They're Hurting, You're Probably Treating Them the Right Way

This is a poignant line from motivational guru Zig Ziglar. Everybody's got something that makes them feel down and out, and those feelings are amplified during the holiday season. One of my older A.A. friends was a fighter pilot during the Vietnam War. December 26th remains one of the hardest days of the year for him. That's because the North Vietnamese would use the Christmas Day cease fire to reset their anti-aircraft batteries each year, and as a result, many of his friends would lose their lives until the new patterns were understood.

You may never know exactly why someone you love is hurting, but if you treat everyone as if they are possibly suffering, as Zig Ziglar points out, you are probably treating them the right way.

Be a pal.

DECEMBER 27
Time to Write Your Year in Review for Next Year

Alcoholics and addicts sometimes get confused over what they are "supposed" to pray for. *The Big Book* suggests that we avoid selfishness, and that we pray for ourselves only in so far as the good things that happen to us can benefit others as well.

This doesn't mean that it's wrong to set goals, and it certainly doesn't mean that we should aim low. While we were drinking and using, we were aiming low. Now that we're clean and sober, it's no longer time to play small. David Dowd, a New York career coach, advises his clients to sit down as the year ends and write a "year in review" of the coming year. In other words, imagine that you are reviewing next year from the perspective of twelve months from now.

What would you like to see happen in that time personally, professionally, financially, spiritually, and in your relationships? Write it all down in the past tense. Don't play small—make this coming year your biggest year ever. You may not get everything you want, but it's hard to move toward a desired outcome until you specify what that outcome should be.

Happy (next) New Year!

DECEMBER 28
When You're Going through Hell, Keep Going

Sometimes we think that once we become sober, nothing bad will ever happen to us again. Sobriety and abstinence don't give us immunity from losses, illness, or other challenges. It's just that now we're not making bad situations worse by drinking, using, or practicing other forms of addictive behavior. Fortunately, the program offers lots of wisdom about how to get through difficult times.

First, *The Big Book* reminds us that we only have one problem—our alcoholism or addiction. Everything else is a situation, and there's a solution for every situation.

Also remember that it says in the Bible, "and it came to pass"—not "and it came to stay."

Every difficult situation has a beginning, a middle…and an end.

As Winston Churchill said,
"When you're going through Hell, keep going."

DECEMBER 29
No Excellence in the Comfort Zone

Life is an unending battle between excellence and comfort. Excellence means that we do things that make us uncomfortable—get through the day sober, make an amend, tell the truth. Comfort means we grab a bowl of ice cream or zone out on social media. There's a time and a place for comfort, but there's no growth—and therefore no excellence—in the comfort zone.

I had the privilege of interviewing Shawn Johnson, the only person to win the gold medal in Olympic women's gymnastics and also first place on *Dancing With the Stars*. I asked her if she simply had a stronger sense of "Eye of the Tiger" than most people.

"No," she said. "I'm just more comfortable being uncomfortable than most people. Most people get frustrated when they're uncomfortable and they quit. I can stay in the uncomfortable place with not being good at something for much longer than anyone else. That's how I'm able to get good at things."

In your life, in the battle between comfort and excellence,
which is winning?

DECEMBER 30
The Last Name of Every
12-Step Program Is…"Anonymous"

At this time of year, we are more likely to spend extended time with family and friends, some of whom are just now discovering that we aren't drinking or using. Remember that you don't owe anyone an explanation for your commitment to a 12-Step program. What you're doing, and why you're doing it, is no one's business. A lot of people out there have mistaken ideas about the 12 Steps and are actually hostile to the whole concept of going to meetings.

The people who are most deeply opposed to your recovery are often the individuals who need the program the most. You don't have to proselytize to them, you don't have to tell them they need to quit drinking or using. Best of all, you don't even need to tell them that you are in the program. Remember, the last half of the name of every 12-Step program is…wait for it…Anonymous. Meaning, your recovery is your business and no one else's.

Mind your own business,
and you won't be minding mine.

DECEMBER 31
Your New Year's Eve
Party Survival Guide

Stay home.

I said it. New Year's Eve for us means just stay home. Old-timers sometimes call New Year's Eve "amateur night" because everybody's out there trying to get drunk, sometimes quickly, sometimes slowly. So that's why we need to be home, tucked safely in our beds, away from all those amateurs who don't know the *first thing* about real drinking.

There's no shame in staying home on New Year's Eve. Roads are clogged with police checkpoints and drunk drivers. When you're sober and you go to a New Year's Eve party, it's embarrassing how desperate everyone looks, relying on alcohol or substitutes in order to have a good time.

Then we remember how we did that, and maybe we stop judging. The short of it is that there's really nothing out there all that special for recovering alcoholics and addicts on December 31. Maybe have a couple of sober friends over, go to an alcathon, or just go to bed early. You've seen the ball drop before. Maybe this is one evening to just sit the whole thing out.

What are you doing on New Year's Eve?
If you're smart, not much.

ABOUT THE AUTHOR

New York Times best selling author "Michael Graubart" has published three books with Hazelden—*Sober Dad, Step Up,* and *Three Simple Rules.* He is a longtime member of Alcoholics Anonymous and Al-Anon and has spent time in various other 12-Step programs. He publishes under a pseudonym in order to remain faithful to the 11th tradition regarding anonymity.

Graubart is also an established singer-songwriter who performs songs from his CDs, *Sober Songs Vol. 1* and *Sober Songs: Boy Meets Girl On A.A. Campus,* at 12-Step conventions and events around the world. Hear the songs and learn more at MichaelGraubart.com. You can reach him via email at SingItSober@gmail.com.

Made in United States
North Haven, CT
10 January 2022